THE ALAMO REMEMBERED

D0840724

# THE ALAMO REMEMBERED

## Tejano Accounts and Perspectives

TIMOTHY M. MATOVINA

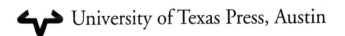 University of Texas Press, Austin

Requests for permission to reproduce material from this work should be sent to Permissions, University of Texas Press, Box 7819, Austin, TX 78713-7819.

∞ The paper used in this publication meets the minimum requirements of American Standard for Information Sciences—Permanence of Paper for Printed Library Materials, ANSI Z39.48-1984.

LIBRARY OF CONGRESS CATALOGING-IN-PUBLICATION DATA
Matovina, Timothy M., 1955–
    The Alamo remembered : Tejano accounts and perspectives / Timothy M. Matovina. — 1st ed.
        p.    cm.
    Includes bibliographical references and index.
ISBN 0-292-75185-0 (cloth), — ISBN 0-292-75186-9 (paper)
    1. Alamo (San Antonio, Tex.)—Siege, 1836.    I. Title.
F390.M485    1995
976.4′351—dc20                                                    95-10131

Front cover photo credits, clockwise from upper left: De Zavala (Adina) Papers, Center for American History, University of Texas at Austin; Courtesy José Antonio Navarro Historical State Park, San Antonio; Courtesy Institute of Texan Cultures, San Antonio; Prints and Photographs Collection, Center for American History, Univeristy of Texas at Austin; Courtesy Institute of Texan Cultures, San Antonio; Courtesy Adolfo C. Herrera and Institute of Texan Cultures, San Antonio; *History of Southwest Texas*, Center for American History, University of Texas at Austin

*To Raphael O'Loughlin, my friend and mentor*

# CONTENTS

ILLUSTRATIONS

The genesis of this book is my earlier study, *Tejano Religion and Ethnicity: San Antonio, 1821–1860* (1995). In that work I examined San Antonio Tejano identity during the decades before and after the Alamo battle. *The Alamo Remembered* expands that earlier analysis by probing the collective legacy of Tejano Alamo accounts. It also presents Tejano Alamo accounts in a single volume for the first time.

Tejano accounts are a frequently untapped resource for historical studies of the Alamo. In her 1931 dissertation, "A Critical Study of the Siege of the Alamo and of the Personnel of Its Defenders," Amelia Williams identified only about half of extant Tejano primary documents. Subsequent works such as John Myers' *The Alamo* (1948), Lon Tinkle's *Thirteen Days to Glory* (1958), Walter Lord's *A Time to Stand* (1961), Jeff Long's *Duel of Eagles* (1990), and Crystal Sasse Ragsdale's *Women and Children of the Alamo* (1994) cited less than a third of the Tejano sources.

In this presentation, I have sectioned the accounts according to four document types: first reports, conversations with local Tejanos, unpublished petitions and depositions, and published accounts. Each document is introduced by a brief statement which identifies the source and the context in which the document was produced. Approximately half of extant Tejano accounts are included; others are omitted because they are repetitive or too brief. All known Tejano sources are cited in the accompanying bibliography and summarized in the introductory essay.

I have not attempted to provide a comprehensive analysis of the historical accuracy in Tejano Alamo accounts, although I amended a few blatant mistakes by inserting corrections in brackets. Given names omitted from original documents are also inserted in brackets, some accompanied by a question mark to indicate that the subject's identity cannot be verified with certainty. The spelling of proper names is standardized to ease recognition of persons mentioned in the various selections. For clarity, some Tejana witnesses are identified by both their maiden and their married names. I also made a few minor editorial changes in spelling and punctuation to render the accounts more readable. Where possible, I transcribed accounts from original documents, but published sources are also cited. Some accounts are excerpts of documents which dealt with events besides the Alamo.

A number of archivists and researchers assisted with the collection of these documents, especially John Ogden Leal, Reynaldo J. Esparza, Vee Gomez, Dorothy Marie Pérez, Kevin R. Young, Stephen L. Hardin, Robert D. Green, Suzette Berry, Jo Myler, Diane Bruce, Thomas Ricks Lindley, Bill Groneman, and Robert M. Benavides. Theresa J. May, Jan McInroy, Sarah Buttrey, and other staff members at the University of Texas Press capably edited and produced the book. I would also like to thank those charged with the care of collections at the General Land Office, Austin; Texas State Archives, Austin; Center for American History, University of Texas, Austin; Library of the University of Texas Institute of Texan Cultures, San Antonio; San Antonio Public Library; Houston Public Library; Library of the University of Texas, San Antonio; Archives, Béxar County Courthouse, San Antonio; Daughters of the Republic of Texas Library, San Antonio; and San Antonio Conservation Society.

Several friends and colleagues offered valuable editorial comments for this volume. These include Martha Ann Kirk, Virgilio Elizondo, Joe J. Bernal, Stephen L. Hardin, Anne A. Fox, Kevin R. Young, Jesús F. de la Teja, Paul Andrew Hutton, Paul D. Lack, and Holly Brear. Elida Yañez helped correct the proof pages. In particular, I thank my good friend Chris Megargee who edited the entire manuscript with an expertise which equals the outstanding assistance he has given me on numerous occasions.

T.M.M.

THE ALAMO REMEMBERED

INTRODUCTION

San Antonians of Mexican heritage frequently recounted their memories of the Alamo; more than seventy-five sources record Tejano testimony. Tejanos gave their testimonies in various contexts. They provided Texan leaders with the first reports of the Alamo's fall and later related details of the interment ceremony for the Alamo defenders. Visitors and newcomers to San Antonio in the decades following the Texas Revolution also reported conversations with local Tejanos about the Alamo. Some later Tejano recollections served the pragmatic purpose of providing testimony for land claims, pension applications, and other petitions for government relief. Other Tejanos published their recollections, two of them just before the Civil War. Around the turn of the century, more than twenty additional Tejano accounts were published, many of them prompted by journalists who desired to preserve eyewitness testimony of the famous battle. These diverse Tejano Alamo documents are important sources for studying the famous battle and its aftermath although, like other accounts, they require critical assessment.

First Reports

On 11 March 1836, Andrés Barcena and Anselmo Bergara arrived in Gonzales (about fifty miles east of San Antonio) and reported that Mexican troops led by General Antonio López de Santa Anna had stormed and taken the Alamo. Although not eyewitnesses, their statements were based on the testimony of Antonio Pérez, who was in San Antonio on 6 March, the day of the final assault. According to Barcena and Bergara, all of the Alamo defenders perished, including seven who surrendered but were executed by order of Santa Anna. The two Tejanos also stated that more than five hundred Mexican soldiers died in the assault and a similar number were wounded. They further claimed that James Bowie was killed while lying sick in bed and that William Barret Travis committed suicide.[1]

A year later, Colonel Juan Nepomuceno Seguín provided an official report of the interment ceremony for the Alamo defenders, whose bodies had been burned at Santa Anna's orders and left in ash heaps near the Alamo. Seguín stated that there were three ash heaps; he had the remains from two of them placed in a coffin. Accompanied by other members of the military, civic authorities, clergy, musicians, and the general populace, he processed with the coffin to San Fernando Church at the center of town and then back to the site of the ash heaps. Soldiers fired three volleys of musketry over the spots of the funeral pyres and the coffin was interred on top of the ashes at the third and largest pyre. Colonel Seguín gave a speech to the crowd in Spanish; Major Thomas Western addressed them in English. In his oration, Seguín stated: "The venerable remains of our worthy companions as witnesses, I invite you to declare to the entire world, 'Texas shall be free and independent, or we shall perish in glorious combat.'"[2]

Conversations with Local Tejanos

San Antonio residents frequently discussed the Alamo with newcomers to the town in the years following the battle. Mary A. Maverick, who moved to San Antonio in 1838, later wrote a brief account of the Alamo which included information from a conversation with Juana Navarro Alsbury. Mirabeau Buonaparte Lamar obtained a list of five Tejano Alamo defenders from Agustín Barrera, a San Antonian who was within the walls of the fortress shortly after its fall. Theodore Gentilz interviewed several local residents before painting two pictures titled *Death of Dickinson* and *Battle of the Alamo*. Reuben M. Potter and John S. Ford did the same before publishing accounts of the battle.[3]

Some visitors to San Antonio recounted conversations with local Tejanos in their journals. An elderly resident of Mexican descent related details of the battle to British traveler William Bollaert and his companions when they toured the Alamo in 1843, for example, and pointed out to them "where

Crockett, Travis, Bowie, and others fell." A Tejana resident also described the horrific battle to Bollaert, as well as the feast day celebrations formerly held at the Alamo mission, the long-past beauty of the mission church, and the merry pealing of its bells which in previous days called local residents to worship. Bemoaning the demise of the mission and its festive celebrations, she stated, "I never look into the ruins of the church without shedding a tear." As if to impress upon him the original purpose of the Alamo, she then presented Bollaert a crucifix made from the stone of the mission. When Josiah Gregg met José Antonio Navarro in 1846, Navarro, who was away at the Convention for Texas Independence when the Alamo fell, "condemned the wonted temerity of the Texans" and asserted that Santa Anna had left the east side of the Alamo unprotected, hoping that the Texans would leave in peace and save the Mexican army a costly victory.[4]

Unpublished Petitions and Depositions

Most Tejano reminiscences of the Alamo from the decades following Texas independence are petitions and depositions filed in land claim cases for heirs of the Alamo defenders. The majority of these documents are sworn testimony that a particular Tejano died in the Alamo fighting on the Texan side. Thus they are an early Tejano rebuttal to depictions of the Alamo defenders as a homogeneous Anglo-American group. In an 1856 deposition, for example, Damasio de los Reyes numbered the Tejano Alamo defenders at seven. Candelario Villanueva testified in 1859 that he entered the Alamo after its fall and saw the bodies of "Gregorio Esparza . . . Antonio Fuentes, Toribio Losoya, Guadalupe Rodríguez, and other Mexicans who had fallen in the defense of the Alamo." Extant land claim files indicate that Tejano citizens sought compensation for the service of seven Tejano Alamo defenders.[5]

Some documents in these files recount personal experiences of individual Tejanos. In his 1859 deposition, Candelario Villanueva stated that his arrival at the Alamo was delayed because Colonel Juan Seguín sent him to lock Seguín's house in the town. While Villanueva performed this task, Mexican troops arrived, cutting off his entry to the Alamo and thus sparing him the fate of its defenders. Francisco Esparza recalled that he sought permission from Mexican general Martín Cos to bury the body of his brother Gregorio. General Cos granted his request, probably because Francisco had fought in the Mexican army during the Texan siege of San Antonio three months earlier and was on reserve with the Mexican forces during their Texas campaign. Because of Francisco's timely action, Gregorio Esparza was the only Alamo defender whose body was not incinerated after the battle. Several Tejano depositions recount that Santa Anna prevailed upon local citizens to burn the bodies of the Alamo defenders after the Mexican victory. Brigidio Guerrero testified that he fought with the Texan army inside the Alamo, but when "he saw that there was no hope left he had the good fortune of saving his life by concealing himself."[6]

A few Tejano reminiscences of the Alamo are recorded in requests other than land claims. In 1850, Gabriel Martínez submitted a claim seeking compensation for a home near the Alamo, along with some corn and clothing, all of which Texas troops had burned during the siege "in order the better to defend said post." Juana Navarro Alsbury's 1857 petition for compensatory relief stated that she rendered "all the service she could towards nursing and attending upon the sick and wounded" inside the Alamo during the siege and that her private property was "seized and taken by the enemy" after the battle.[7]

Published Accounts

The first published Tejano account dealing with the Alamo battle was Juan Seguín's 1858 memoir. Seguín was among the Alamo defenders but left the fort to seek reinforcements. His account details his futile efforts to enlist the support of Colonel James Walker Fannin and his troops, as well as Seguín's return to San Antonio on 6 March with provisions for the Alamo defenders, only to find that the garrison had already fallen.[8]

Two years later, Francisco Antonio Ruiz recorded the first published Tejano account of the battle itself in an entry of *The Texas Almanac for 1860*. Ruiz was the mayor of San Antonio when the Alamo fell, and Santa Anna ordered him to remove the dead after the battle. His account, titled "Fall of the Alamo, and Massacre of Travis and His Brave Associates," describes the battle, the gallantry of the Texan soldiers, the incineration of their bodies at Santa Anna's orders, and the disposal of corpses in the San

Antonio River because the numbers of deceased Mexican soldiers made it impossible to bury them all.[9]

Extant sources indicate that no further Tejano accounts were published for nearly thirty years. As the remaining eyewitnesses dwindled to a precious few, however, newspaper reporters and others began to record Tejano reminiscences of the Alamo with some regularity. These reminiscences provide more vivid detail than earlier reports, petitions, depositions, and conversations recorded in travelogues. They also reflect the diversity of vantage points from which Tejanos observed the siege of the Alamo, the battle, and its aftermath. Some Tejanos witnessed these events from within the Alamo, some left the garrison as couriers or scouts, some watched from the distance in the town, and others left San Antonio during the hostilities, returning after the battle was over.

Particularly vivid accounts of the battle itself are attributed to three observers from within the Alamo: Juana Navarro Alsbury, Enrique Esparza, and Andrea Castañón Villanueva, more popularly known as Madam Candelaria. They describe details such as the surging columns of Mexican troops and the heroic deeds of Crockett, Bowie, and Travis. Esparza, who was a boy at the time, also relates that his father, Gregorio, fought valiantly as an Alamo defender and died near the cannon that he tended.[10]

A prominent contribution of the Navarro Alsbury and Esparza accounts is that they recall those who survived the final assault. While the lists of survivors in these accounts are inconsistent, cumulatively they include Juana's son Alejo Pérez and her sister Gertrudis Navarro; Enrique's mother, Anna Salazar Esparza, his sister, and three brothers; Mrs. Concepción Losoya, her daughter, and two sons; Mrs. Victoriana and three little girls; Mrs. Susanna Dickinson and her baby; an old woman named Petra; Mrs. Juana Melton; Trinidad Saucedo; and others who are not identified by name.[11] Esparza also attests that Brigidio Guerrero was spared because he convinced Mexican soldiers that the Texan forces were holding him prisoner.

In addition, Esparza recounts the traumatic experience of the survivors after the battle. He states that Mexican soldiers fired several volleys into the room where he and others were concealed, killing a young boy. Then the soldiers entered the room and demanded the Texans' money. When they realized that no booty was forthcoming, they took the women and children to the home of Ramón Músquiz, a prominent San Antonio political figure. Músquiz ensured that the prisoners were fed. Several hours later the soldiers led them before Santa Anna, who exacted an oath of allegiance from them before giving each woman a blanket and two silver dollars. After this interview, the Alamo survivors were free to go.

Accounts from defenders who left the Alamo as couriers or scouts include those of Juan Seguín and Trinidad Coy. As was previously mentioned, Seguín stated in his 1858 memoirs that he left the Alamo to seek reinforcements for the beleaguered fortress. In two later accounts, he described in greater detail the danger entailed in his departure from the Alamo. Trinidad Coy's amazing story was reported by his son Andrés in a 1911 interview. The younger Coy recollected that his father was one of several scouts sent from the Alamo to ascertain Santa Anna's position and intentions. After many days of searching, a farmer advised him that the Mexican troops were only a few miles away and were headed for San Antonio. Immediately Coy set out for the Alamo, but his horse refused to move. Upon inquiry, Coy discovered that a young boy had unwittingly grazed the horse in a corral filled with "loco weed." The boy offered a "wiry little pony" to replace Coy's sick horse, but this mount proved inadequate. Mexican soldiers soon spotted Coy and the pony fell over dead when Coy tried to outrun them. Taken as a prisoner to San Antonio, Coy witnessed the movements of the Mexican troops from afar. Finally he was able to escape and work his way to the Alamo, only to discover the funeral pyre which contained the burning remains of his fallen comrades.[12]

Eulalia Yorba, María de Jesús Delgado Buquor, Juan Díaz, and Juan Vargas remained in the town during the siege and fall of the Alamo and thus observed the battle from a distance. Yorba attended the sick within the Alamo immediately after it fell; her account includes her poignant memories of the battle's aftermath. Delgado Buquor and Díaz were children at the time and apparently did not venture out of the town, but they did see the rising smoke from the funeral pyres. Mexican troops impressed Vargas to serve in their camp, which was close enough to the Alamo for him to hear the sounds of the battle.[13]

A significant element of these accounts is that they reveal how the Mexican troops treated San Antonio residents. Yorba recalled that Mexican soldiers confiscated all the food in her home but promised her that she and her children would not be harmed if they remained in the house. She went to the rectory of the local priest seeking food and comfort and from there saw the final assault. Delgado Buquor stated that Mexican soldiers forced her family from their home and treated them harshly. She also related that Santa Anna seized a young girl from her neighborhood and held her captive while the Mexican troops were in San Antonio. Díaz, whose father was the custodian of San Fernando parish, recounted that many Mexican officers stayed at the church. Since his mother fed them, Santa Anna ordered his soldiers to guard their home. Perhaps because of this protection, Díaz recollected "but few cases of damage" resulting from the depredations of Santa Anna's soldiers. Vargas remembered that Santa Anna's troops confiscated local supplies and even threatened him with execution when he refused to participate in the storming of the Alamo. Instead, they compelled him to carry equipage, perform kitchen duties, assist the wounded, and bury their dead.

Other San Antonians abandoned the town during the hostilities but later recorded their memories of the events before and after the battle. Pablo Díaz recalled the fortifications which the Texan soldiers made at the Alamo in preparation for Santa Anna's arrival. He also described the funeral pyres of the Alamo defenders after the battle, along with the gruesome spectacle of Mexican corpses floating in the river. Juan Antonio Chávez, who was a boy at the time, fled with his family but returned in time to see the incinerated bodies of the Alamo defenders. Another childhood witness, José María Rodríguez, stated that his father advised Colonel Travis to retreat from San Antonio before Santa Anna's forces overwhelmed him, but Travis did not believe that Santa Anna could mount so large an army only three months after the Texas volunteers conquered San Antonio. Afterward Rodríguez's father left San Antonio to join General Sam Houston's army, and his mother took the family to a nearby ranch. From the rooftop of a house, the young Rodríguez saw the flash of guns and heard the boom of cannons during the Alamo battle. Yet another Tejano who left San Antonio before the Mexican army occupied the town was Antonio Menchaca. Menchaca's memoirs relate details such as the arrival of Davy Crockett and his Tennessee volunteers at San Antonio, the first courier's report of Santa Anna's advancing army, Menchaca's flight from the town with his family, and his conscription into the Texan army by General Edward Burleson at Gonzales.[14]

Tejano Accounts and Historical Studies of the Alamo

Like other Alamo accounts, Tejano accounts require critical assessment. Historians must bear in mind that petitions for land claims, pensions, and other government compensation are legal documents that reflect their authors' purposes of procuring their claims. Statements like those of Andrés Barcena, Anselmo Bergara, and José Antonio Navarro were based on second-hand information and could reflect inaccurate renderings of eyewitness testimony. Furthermore, third parties recorded their statements, removing extant documents one step further from the original sources. Some Tejano testimony may also suffer from mistakes in translation. Anglo Americans interviewed many witnesses in Spanish, at times with the help of an interpreter. Significant observations and details could easily have been lost or misunderstood in the process.[15]

Published Tejano accounts merit the most critical attention, since the majority of them were based on interviews conducted at least fifty years after the recorded events and many of the witnesses were children at the time of the battle. The published accounts also tend to provide far more detail than other Tejano testimony. Such detailed accounts are more prone to inaccuracies than the general observations contained in earlier statements. The position from which eyewitnesses viewed the siege and battle is yet another consideration in assessing the veracity of their accounts, since the precision of their descriptions is contingent on how clearly they saw these events.

Interviewer bias also undoubtedly influenced how reporters recorded Tejano testimony. In a 1902 article, for example, a *San Antonio Express* reporter asserted that Enrique Esparza "tells a straight story. Although he is a Mexican, his gentleness and unassuming frankness are like the typical old Texan." The presumption that Mexicans tend not to tell "straight stories" reveals the racial bias of this reporter, a bias that easily could have influenced an interview of Esparza or other Tejanos.[16]

While a comprehensive analysis of the historical accuracy in Tejano Alamo accounts is beyond the scope of this work, the possibilities of errant observation, alterations in original testimony by second or third parties, faulty translation, memory lapse, and interviewer bias indicate the need for critical assessment in studies that utilize Tejano (and other) sources. Despite this need, extant Tejano accounts remain a significant and often untapped resource for historical studies of the Alamo.

NOTES

1. "Examination of Andrés Barcena and Anselmo Bergara," Gonzales, 11 March 1836, in *The Papers of the Texas Revolution, 1835–1836*, ed. John H. Jenkins (Austin: Presidial, 1973), 5:45–46; E. N. Gray to [?], 11 March 1836 (typescript), Republic of Texas General File, Center for American History, University of Texas, Austin (CAH); Sam Houston to James W. Fannin, 11 March 1836, in *Papers of the Texas Revolution*, ed. Jenkins, 5:52–54. The examination of Barcena and Bergara and E. N. Gray's letter are the first two documents in this collection. Hereafter the document number of sources contained in the collection are cited in brackets. For the examination of Barcena and Bergara, see also *Texas Letters*, ed. Frederick C. Chabot (San Antonio: Yanaguana Society, 1940), 146–147; Gray's letter is in *Papers of the Texas Revolution*, ed. Jenkins, 5:48–49; Houston's letter is also in *The Writings of Sam Houston, 1813–1863*, ed. Amelia W. Williams and Eugene C. Barker (Austin: University of Texas Press, 1938; reprint, Austin: Pemberton, 1970), 1:362–365. After Barcena and Bergara arrived in Gonzales, Juan Seguín reportedly advised Francisco Ruiz and José Antonio Navarro that the Alamo had fallen. I have not yet located this correspondence. William F. Gray, *From Virginia to Texas, 1835; Diary of Col. Wm. F. Gray, Giving Details of His Journey to Texas and Return in 1835–1836 and Second Journey to Texas in 1837* (Houston: Gray, Dillaye, 1909; reprint, Houston: Fletcher Young, 1965), 131.

2. Juan Seguín to General Albert Sidney Johnston, 13 March 1837, Johnston Papers, Howard Tilton Memorial Library, Tulane University, New Orleans, [3]; *Columbia* (later *Houston*) *Telegraph and Texas Register*, 28 March, 4 April 1837 (quotation), [4]. Seguín's speech and letter are also in *A Revolution Remembered: The Memoirs and Selected Correspondence of Juan N. Seguín*, ed. Jesús F. de la Teja (Austin: State House Press, 1991), 156, 161–162.

3. Mary A. Maverick, "Fall of the Alamo," in *Samuel Maverick, Texan: 1803–1870. A Collection of Letters, Journals, and Memoirs*, ed. Rena Maverick Green (San Antonio: Privately printed, 1952), 55–56; Agustín Barrera,

"Mexicans Who Fell in the Alamo," 184–?, in *The Papers of Mirabeau Buonaparte Lamar*, ed. Charles Adams Gulick, Jr., and Katherine Elliott (Austin: Von Boeckmann-Jones, 1973), 6:297; Agustín Barrera, Deposition, 26 July 1856, Carlos Espalier File, Memorials and Petitions, Texas State Archives, Austin (TSA); Damasio de los Reyes, Deposition, 4 September 1856, Court of Claims Voucher File #6073, General Land Office, Austin (GLO), [9]; Agustín Barrera, Deposition, 16 April 1861, Court of Claims Voucher File #5026, GLO; Antonio Cruz Arocha, Statement, no date, Gentilz Papers, Daughters of the Republic of Texas Library, San Antonio, [7]; *Gentilz: Artist of the Old Southwest* (Austin: University of Texas Press, 1974), 22; Reuben M. Potter, *The Fall of the Alamo* (Hillsdale, New Jersey: Otterden, 1977), 11–12, 38, 46 (reprinted from *Magazine of American History* 2 [January 1878]: 1–21); John S. Ford, "The Alamo's Fall: A Synopsis of the Display of Heroism," *San Antonio Express*, 6 March 1889, 2; Ford, "The Fall of the Alamo," *Dallas Morning News*, 12 November 1892, 6; Ford, *Origin and Fall of the Alamo March 6, 1836* (San Antonio: Johnson Brothers, 1895), 22. Potter's account originally appeared in the *San Antonio Herald* in 1860. *Alamo Express* (San Antonio), 18 August 1860, 3.

4. William Bollaert, *William Bollaert's Texas*, ed. W. Eugene Hollon and Ruth Lapham Butler (Norman: University of Oklahoma Press, 1956), 222–224, [5]; José Antonio Navarro, in Josiah Gregg, *Diary and Letters of Josiah Gregg*, ed. Maurice Garland Fulton, with an introduction by Paul Horgan (Norman: University of Oklahoma Press, 1941), 1:232, [6].

5. De los Reyes, Deposition; Candelario Villanueva, Deposition, 26 August 1859, Court of Claims Voucher File #2558, GLO, [12]. See also Court of Claims Voucher File #3416, 1861, GLO; Court of Claims Voucher File #5026, 1861, GLO; Luz Guarde Grande, Petition, 5 October 1855, Carlos Espalier File, Memorials and Petitions, TSA; Antonio Fuentes File, 1856, Memorials and Petitions, TSA; Juan Jiménez and Gertrudes Jiménez, Petition, 2 February 1861, Damacio Jiménez File, Headright Book 2, 370, Archives, Béxar County Courthouse, San Antonio (ABCC). For the latter petition, see also Raul Casso IV, "Damacio Jiménez: The Lost and Found Alamo Defender," *Southwestern Historical Quarterly* 96 (July 1992): 86–92. Except for Guadalupe Rodríguez, all of the Tejanos mentioned in these files are included on the official list of defenders at the Alamo.

6. Villanueva, Deposition; Francisco Esparza, Deposition, 26 August

1859, Court of Claims Voucher File #2558, GLO [11]; De los Reyes, Deposition; Francisco Antonio Ruiz, Deposition, 16 April 1861, Court of Claims Voucher File #5026, GLO [14]; Cornelio Delgado, Deposition, 30 March 1861, Damacio Jiménez File, Headright Book 2, 371–372, ABCC; Brigidio Guerrero, Petition, 4 January 1861, Court of Claims Voucher File #3416, GLO [13].

7. Gabriel Martínez, Petition, 1 January 1850, Memorials and Petitions, TSA, [8]; Juana Navarro Alsbury, Petition, 1 November 1857, Memorials and Petitions, TSA, [10].

8. Juan N. Seguín, *Personal Memoirs of John N. Seguín from the Year 1834 to the Retreat of General Woll from the City of San Antonio in 1842* (San Antonio: Ledger Book and Job Office, 1858), 8–10, [15]. This section of Seguín's memoirs is also in *A Revolution Remembered*, ed. De la Teja, 79–81, 107–108.

9. Francis Antonio Ruiz, "Fall of the Alamo, and Massacre of Travis and His Brave Associates," in *The Texas Almanac for 1860*, trans. J[osé] A[gustín] Quintero (Houston: James Burke, 1859), 80–81, [16]. Also in *The Texas Almanac, 1857–1873: A Compendium of Texas History*, comp. James M. Day, with an introduction by Walter Moore (Waco: Texian Press, 1967), 356–358; *Alamo Express* (San Antonio), 25 August 1860, 1.

10. Juana Navarro Alsbury, "Mrs. Alsbury's Recollections of the Alamo," c. 1880s, in "John S. Ford Memoirs" (unpublished manuscript), 102–104, CAH, [17]; Enrique Esparza, interviewed in "Another Child of the Alamo," Adina De Zavala, *San Antonio Light*, 10 November 1901, 9, [23]; Esparza, interviewed in "The Story of Enrique Esparza," *San Antonio Express*, 22 November 1902, 8, [24]; Esparza, interviewed in "Alamo's Only Survivor," Charles Merritt Barnes, *San Antonio Express*, 12 May 1907, 14; 19 May 1907, 47, [26]; Esparza, interviewed in "Alamo's Fall Is Told by Witness in a Land Suit," *San Antonio Express*, 9 December 1908, 20; Barnes, *Combats and Conquests of Immortal Heroes: Sung in Song and Told in Story* (San Antonio: Guessaz & Ferlet, 1910), 227; Barnes, "Builders' Spades Turn Up Soil Baked by Alamo Funeral Pyres," *San Antonio Express*, 26 March 1911, 26, [32]; Barnes, "Men Still Living Who Saw the Fall of the Alamo," *San Antonio Express*, 27 August 1911, 9, [33]; Esparza, in "Esparza, the Boy of the Alamo, Remembers," in *Rise of the Lone Star: A Story of Texas Told by Its Pioneers*, ed. Howard R. Driggs and Sarah S. King (New York: Frederick

A. Stokes, 1936), 215, 220–230; Andrea Castañón Villanueva, interviewed in "Señora Candelaria," in *San Antonio de Béxar: A Guide and History*, ed. and comp. William Corner (San Antonio: Bainbridge & Corner, 1890; reprint, San Antonio: Graphic Arts, 1977), 117–119; Castañón Villanueva, interviewed in "Fall of the Alamo," *San Antonio Express*, 6 March 1892, 6, [20]; Castañón Villanueva, interviewed in "The Last Survivor of the Alamo, Señora Candelaria," Lee C. Harby, *Times-Democrat* (New Orleans), 22 April 1894, 28; Castañón Villanueva, interviewed in "The Last Voice Hushed," *San Antonio Express*, 11 February 1899, 5; Castañón Villanueva, interviewed in "Alamo Massacre," *San Antonio Light*, 19 February 1899, 6, [22]. See also Maurice Elfer, *Madam Candelaria: Unsung Heroine of the Alamo* (Houston: Rein, 1933). Unlike other accounts cited in this section, the Navarro Alsbury account has not previously been published. It is included here because, like many published accounts of this period, it is a relatively extensive narrative obtained by an interviewer.

11. Some names of survivors are spelled differently in the various accounts.

12. Seguín, interviewed in "Colonel Juan N. Seguín," *Clarksville Standard*, 4 March 1887, [18]; Seguín to William Winston Fontaine, 7 June 1890, W. W. Fontaine Collection, CAH, [19]; Trinidad Coy, interview of his son Andrés Coy in "New Light on Alamo Massacre," *San Antonio Light*, 26 November 1911, 41, [34]. These Seguín accounts are also in *A Revolution Remembered*, ed. De la Teja, 191–195.

13. Eulalia Yorba, interviewed in "Another Story of the Alamo," *San Antonio Express*, 12 April 1896, 13, [21]; María de Jesús Delgado Buquor, interviewed in "Witnessed Last Struggle of the Alamo Patriots," *San Antonio Express*, 19 July 1907, 3, [27]; Juan Díaz, interviewed in "As a Boy, Juan Díaz, Venerable San Antonian Witnessed the Attack on the Alamo," *San Antonio Light*, 1 September 1907, 13, [28]; Barnes, "Men Still Living Who Saw the Fall"; Juan Vargas, interviewed in "This Man Was Old When Santa Anna Spilled Blood in Alamo and Built Texans' Funeral Pyre," Louis de Nette, *San Antonio Light*, 3 April 1910, 34, [31]. Juan E. Barrera is another Tejano who was in San Antonio when Santa Anna's army arrived. Although no Barrera account is extant, a brief recollection attributed to him is in Barnes, *Combats and Conquests*, 231.

14. Pablo Díaz, interviewed in "Aged Citizen Describes Alamo Fight

and Fire," Charles Merritt Barnes, *San Antonio Express*, 1 July 1906, 11, [25]; Díaz, interviewed in "This Man Heard Shots Fired at Battle of Alamo," *San Antonio Light*, 31 October 1909, 10, [30]; Barnes, "Builders' Spades Turn Up Soil"; Juan Antonio Chávez, interviewed in "Remembers Early Days," Barnes, *San Antonio Express*, 15 December 1907, 54; 22 December 1907, 11, [29]; Barnes, *Combats and Conquests*, 218; Barnes, "Men Still Living Who Saw the Fall"; Chávez, interviewed in "Bullet-Ridden and Tomahawk-Scarred San Antonio Home Is Being Demolished," *San Antonio Express*, 19 April 1914, B45, [36]; J[osé] M[aría] Rodríguez, interviewed in "Stirring Events Are Remembered by Texas Jurist," *San Antonio Express*, 8 September 1912, 35; Rodríguez, *Rodríguez Memoirs of Early Texas* (San Antonio: Passing Show Printing, 1913; reprint, San Antonio: Standard, 1961), 7–9, 16, 71, [35]; Antonio Menchaca, *Memoirs*, with a foreword by Frederick C. Chabot and an introduction by James P. Newcomb (San Antonio: Yanaguana Society, 1937), 22–23, [37]. A slightly different rendering of Menchaca's memoirs is in "The Memoirs of Captain Menchaca, 1807–1836" (typescript), ed. and annot. James P. Newcomb, 3–7, CAH. The original of Menchaca's memoirs is also at CAH, although it lacks the pages cited here. This original document is not dated but precedes Menchaca's 1879 death. The decision to abandon San Antonio during hostilities was undoubtedly influenced by Tejano recollections of cruelty and bloodshed during 1811–1813 revolutionary battles in their hometown. Records of such recollections are in Rodríguez, *Memoirs*, 59; Menchaca, *Memoirs*, 13–19; José Antonio Navarro, "José Antonio Navarro, Béxar, [Texas]," 18 May 1841, in *Papers of Lamar*, ed. Gulick and Elliott, 3:525–527; Navarro, "José Antonio Navarro San Antonio de Béxar? [Texas], Autobiographical Notes," [1841?], in *Papers of Lamar*, ed. Gulick and Elliott, 3:597–598; Navarro, *Apuntes históricos interesantes de San Antonio de Béxar escritos por el C. Dn. José Antonio Navarro, en noviembre de 1853. Y publicados por varios de sus amigos* (San Antonio: Privately printed, 1869), 4–20. Navarro's account in the latter work originally appeared in four newspaper installments: *Western Texan* (San Antonio), 1 December 1853; *San Antonio Ledger*, 12, 19 December 1857, 2 January 1858. The 1853 installment is also in "Anonymous. Early History of San Antonio," 1 December 1853, in Gulick and Elliott, eds., *Papers of Lamar*, 4:5–12. Navarro's *Apuntes* are republished in David R. McDonald and Timothy M. Matovina, eds., *Defending*

*Mexican Valor in Texas: José Antonio Navarro's Historical Writings, 1853-1857* (Austin: State House Press, 1995).

15. For interviews conducted in Spanish, see, for example, José Antonio Navarro, in Gregg, *Diary and Letters of Josiah Gregg*, ed. Fulton, 1:232; Esparza, in "The Story of Enrique Esparza"; Castañón Villanueva, in "Señora Candelaria," in Corner, ed. and comp., *San Antonio de Béxar*, 117, 119; Castañón Villanueva, in "Fall of the Alamo"; Pablo Díaz, in "Aged Citizen Describes Alamo Fight and Fire," Barnes; Díaz, in "This Man Heard Shots Fired at Battle of Alamo."

16. Esparza, interviewed in "The Story of Enrique Esparza."

FIRST REPORTS

Andrés Barcena and Anselmo Bergara
  Examination by Texas Military Officials
  GONZALES, II MARCH 1836

*Andrés Barcena and Anselmo Bergara fled from the hostilities in the San Antonio area and brought the first report of the Alamo's fall to settlements east of there. Although they were not eyewitnesses, their statements were based on the testimony of Antonio Pérez, who was in San Antonio on 6 March, the day of the final assault. These statements are in the handwriting of Colonel George Washington Hockley, General Sam Houston's chief of staff.*

Andrés Barcena says that last Saturday night Anselmo Bergara arrived at the rancho of Don José Flores, where he who declares was and that Bergara informed him that his mother had solicited him Bergara to take her son if he could find him to the Colorado River to avoid the military who were gathering up all they could and making soldiers of them.

Antonio Pérez left the rancho of Don José María Arocha on Sunday morning last and returned in the evening with the notice that the soldiers of Santa Anna had that morning entered the Alamo and killed all the men who were inside and that he saw about five hundred of the Mexican soldiers that had been killed and as many wounded.

Bergara landed at the rancho Saturday evening and gave no notice of the fall of the Alamo, but that Antonio Pérez brought the news to the rancho Sunday evening, and Father [?] Bergara stated at the rancho that [Ramón] Músquiz had advised him to leave as it was not prudent for him to remain.

Antonio Pérez was called to Béxar by Don Luciano Navarro for the purpose of sending him to Gonzales with a letter calling on all Mexicans to come forward and present themselves to the President to receive their pardon and enter on their own proper pursuits. Antonio refused to come unless Santa Anna would give a passport which could not then be obtained but was promised in three or four days and that on tomorrow if he (Antonio) comes he will leave the rancho for this place.

General [Martín] Cos entered Béxar with seven hundred men (so says Bergara).

Andrés Barcena and Anselmo Bergara
>   Letter of E. N. Gray
>   11 MARCH 1836

*E. N. Gray summarized the testimony of Andrés Barcena and Anselmo Bergara the same day that George Washington Hockley recorded their statements (see document 1). Gray's correspondence narrates additional details from the Tejanos' testimony of the final assault.*

At four o'clock this afternoon, Anselmo Bergara and Andrew Bargana [Barcena] came to this town [Gonzales] with the disagreeable intelligence of the taking of the Alamo by General Santa Anna. The event is related in the following manner: On Saturday night, the 5th of the present month, he marched his infantry under the walls and surrounded them with cavalry to prevent escape in case they should attempt to fly. At daybreak on Sunday morning he planted his ladders, which were carried by the infantry, against the sides of the four walls and carried the place by assault with great loss of infantry. All within the fort perished. Seven of them were killed by order of Santa Anna when in the act of giving up their arms. Travis killed himself. And Bowie was killed while lying sick in bed. The Misses [Juana Navarro Alsbury?] and [Gertrudis Navarro?], who were in the fort, were delivered up to their father.

All the above is derived from what was told to Bergara by D[on Antonio Pérez?] on Sunday night when he, Bergara, went in from the country. On the morning of the attack he had come hastily out to the country. It must be understood that Bergara remained at large in Béxar thirteen days after the entrance of Santa Anna and walked about undisturbed by him all that time.

Barcena says that Bergara came to the rancho of my [his] father-in-law on Saturday night, before the entrance of the troops into the walls, and that he knows nothing about it—only what was told by Antonio Pérez who came from Béxar (where he had been called by D[on?] L[uciano Navarro?]) on Sunday in the night, who said that he had been in the battle—that 521 of the infantry were killed and as many more badly wounded.

The contradiction of these two men makes me suspect that they are spies sent by Santa Anna—because, why should Bergara fly from Béxar after remaining so many days there undisturbed and enjoying himself?

Juan Nepomuceno Seguín.
Courtesy Institute of Texan
Cultures, San Antonio.
Original painting at Texas
State Archives, Austin.

- 3 -

Juan N. Seguín
    Letter to General
    Albert Sidney Johnston
    13 MARCH 1837

*After the victory at San Jacinto (21 April 1836) established Texas independence, Colonel Juan Nepomuceno Seguín commanded a small troop charged to defend the new Republic's western frontier. Seguín and his force occupied San Antonio for four months beginning in November 1836. Before leaving the city, he led the interment ceremony for the Alamo defenders and provided an official report of its proceedings. Since Seguín's knowledge of English was limited, he employed an interpreter to draft his official correspondence, including this letter.*

In conformity with the orders from General Felix Huston dated some time back, I caused the honors of war to be paid to the remains of the heroes of Alamo on the 25th of February last. The ashes were found in three heaps. I caused a coffin to be prepared neatly covered with black, the ashes from the two smallest heaps were placed therein and with a view to attach additional solemnity to the occasion were carried to the parish church in Béxar whence it moved with the procession at four o'clock on the afternoon of the day above mentioned. The procession passed through the principal street of the city, crossed the river and passing through the principal avenue arrived at the spot whence part of the ashes had been collected, the procession halted, the coffin was placed upon the spot and three volleys of musquetry were discharged over it by one of the companies, proceeding onwards to the second spot from whence the ashes were taken where the same honors were done and thence to the principal spot and place of interment, the coffin was then placed upon the large heap of ashes when I addressed a few words to the battalion and assemblage present in honor of the occasion in the Castilian language as I do not possess the English. Major [Thomas] Western then addressed the concourse in the latter tongue, the coffin and all the ashes were then interred and three volleys of musquetry were fired over the grave by the whole battalion with an accuracy that would do honor to the best disciplined troops. We then marched back to quarter in the city with music and colors flying. Half hour guns were not fired because I had no powder for the purpose, but every honor was done within the reach of my scanty means. I hope as a whole my efforts may meet your approbation.

- 4 -

Juan N. Seguín
   *Columbia* (later *Houston*) *Telegraph and Texas Register*
   4 APRIL 1837

*Colonel Juan Nepomuceno Seguín gave a speech in Spanish at the interment ceremony for the Alamo defenders (see document 3). This oration was translated and published in a Texas newspaper.*

Companions in Arms!! These remains which we have the honor of carrying on our shoulders are those of the valiant heroes who died in the Alamo. Yes, my friends, they preferred to die a thousand times rather than submit themselves to the tyrant's yoke. What a brilliant example! Deserving of being noted in the pages of history. The spirit of liberty appears to be looking out from its elevated throne with its pleasing mien and pointing to us, saying: "There are your brothers, Travis, Bowie, Crockett, and others whose valor places them in the rank of my heroes." Yes soldiers and fellow citizens, these are the worthy beings who, by the twists of fate, during the present campaign delivered their bodies to the ferocity of their enemies; who, barbarously treated as beasts, were bound by their feet and dragged to this spot, where they were reduced to ashes. The venerable remains of our worthy companions as witnesses, I invite you to declare to the entire world, "Texas shall be free and independent or we shall perish in glorious combat."

CONVERSATIONS WITH LOCAL TEJANOS

- 5 -

Anonymous Local Tejanos
  Diary of William Bollaert
  19–20 SEPTEMBER 1843

*During his 1843 visit to San Antonio, British traveler William Bollaert visited
with two Tejanos at the Alamo, one a woman who had lived near the Alamo
since her childhood. Afterward he recounted their conversations in his diary.*

September 19th, 1843 . . . In the evening a party was made up to visit the
Alamo, passing the wooden bridge which is out of repair owing to a swell
in the river. The sanguinary histories connected with this spot we all knew,
but we met with an old Mexican who, as he traversed this sacred pile of
ruin with us, showed us where Crockett, Travis, Bowie, and others fell,
recounting to us the brutalities of Santa Anna and his followers. One thing
in particular our guide expatiated upon, namely the execution Travis did
with "his gun" upon the Toluca regiment. . . .

September 20th, 1843. On going to the Alamo to make sketches, an old
Mexican woman kindly brought me out a small chair and table. She had
lived near the "Alamo" from a child and had known nearly all those who
had fallen in the wars. "Yes Sir," said she. "I knew them all. Poor Travis!
What a tiger Santa Anna must have been. I shed many a tear during that
siege. He can have no peace." Whilst she was recounting the horrors of the
siege, I was sketching and sympathizing with her, when she looked over
my shoulder. "Ah Señor, had you but seen the Alamo on a feast day, as I
have seen it, not like it is now, in ruins, you would have been delighted and
I would not leave my old rancho here for the best house in San Antonio."
She flattered my drawing as it went on and resumed her observations: "Then
did I go every morning to Mass with old Aunt Carmelita, who was one of
a very few who escaped the *matanza* [massacre] by the Comanches at San
Sabá (she only died a few years since), but now I only go into town on
Sunday and great feast days. Ah! Señor, the front of the church was so
beautiful. On one side of the doorway stood San Antonio, on the other
San Fernando with other saints. The bells rung a merry peal; they were
broken up and thrown into the river, some say fifty quintals weight (five
thousand lbs.), the enemy not being able to melt them into bullets. I never
look into the ruins of the church without shedding a tear; not half the

walls are now to be seen and those grown over with weeds, moss, and even shrubs growing out of the cracks in its walls and what numbers of bats and snakes, but I have seen the Texas flag float over the poor old walls. It was then all walled in. There were large barracks for the troops and gardens with fruit trees, vegetables, and flowers in the *labores* [fields]."

The old lady stopped her lamentations and looking at the sketch [added]: "Ah, there is nearly all but the old walls and ruins behind. Well, well, I am glad you love the Alamo; here, I'll give you a crucifix made from the stone. Tis but ill-done but will serve as a remembrance of the Alamo." On my return I showed her the sketch of San Antonio. "Very good, but you see it is in ruins and will remain so—*hasta quien sabe* until who knows when!"

*José Antonio Navarro.*
*Courtesy José Antonio*
*Navarro State Historical*
*Park, San Antonio.*

- 6 -

José Antonio Navarro
Diary of Josiah Gregg
23 SEPTEMBER 1846

*During his 1846 visit to San Antonio, entrepreneur Josiah Gregg met José Antonio Navarro, a prominent San Antonio merchant, land investor, and political figure. Although Navarro was away at the Convention for Texas Independence when the Alamo fell, he commented on the temerity of Texan Alamo defenders. Gregg's diary contains a translated synopsis of his Spanish conversation with Navarro.*

September 23, 1846 . . . Not very long after my arrival at San Antonio de Béxar, I visited Don José Antonio Navarro . . . He with much justice condemned the wonted temerity of the Texans which, as he remarked, had cost them a great deal of blood and most of their defeats. He instanced, in particular, the affair of the Alamo, where 180 odd men undertook to defend it against several thousand. He asserted that Santa Anna at all times left the eastern side of the fortification free, in hopes the Texans would escape—preferring to let them go in peace to a victory over them which he knew must cost him dearly.

- 7 -

Antonio Cruz Arocha
Papers of Theodore Gentilz
NO DATE

*French artist Theodore Gentilz, who first visited San Antonio in 1844, interviewed several local residents before painting two pictures titled* Death of Dickinson *and* Battle of the Alamo. *His notes from these interviews include the statement of Antonio Cruz Arocha. Originally recorded in French, this statement is presented here as translated by Pascal Wilkins.*

Colonel Juan Nepomuceno Seguín escaped from the Alamo [during] the night by the *acequia* [canal], Cruz was waiting for him with a horse from a *jacal* [hut] [on the] west side in front of the church. Cruz lived in one of the *jacales* in the vicinity of the place of San [Antonio de] Valero. His wife, Doña María Jesusa Peña, could see by a small window all or a good part of what happened. After the firing ceased, Santa Anna got in by the southwest door. A few Texans which were hidden came to kneel down before him, holding each a little white flag (*banderita blanca*). The *Mochos* [soldiers?] surrounding them were hesitating as to kill them but Santa Anna going by made a signal by his head and sword and immediately they were pierced by bayonets.

UNPUBLISHED PETITIONS AND DEPOSITIONS

- 8 -

Gabriel Martínez
    Petition
    1 JANUARY 1850

*Texas veteran Gabriel Martínez submitted a claim seeking compensation for a home near the Alamo, along with some corn and clothing, all of which Texas troops had burned during their defense of the Alamo.*

State of Texas, County of Béxar

Gabriel Martínez, native and citizen of San Antonio, under oath declares that on or about the 28th day of February A.D. 1836 Colonel William B. Travis, then in command of the forces of Texas, besieged in the Alamo at Béxar by the Mexican forces under General Santa Anna, in order the better to defend said post of the Alamo, did order to be burned or destroyed the following described property of said Gabriel Martínez; to wit, one *jacal* [hut] about six varas square situated on the east side of Alamo Street at the corner of the Plaza de Valero, near the Alamo; said house containing some clothes and about thirty-six *fanegas* [bushels] of corn, the whole valued at about $170.00. G. Martínez [the] aforesaid further declares that although said property was destroyed by order of the authorized agent of the Government of Texas that he has never served against said government, but served said government as soldier under the command of Colonel J[ohn] C[offee] Hays for the space of about three years, nevertheless he has never received from said Government of Texas any compensation for the loss sustained as above mentioned. Whereupon he declares he is justly entitled to compensation to said amount of $170.00 from said Government of Texas.

- 9 -
Damasio de los Reyes
    Deposition
    4 SEPTEMBER 1856

*Damasio de los Reyes filed a deposition to support the land grant petition of Andrés Nava's heirs. De los Reyes testified that Nava was one of seven Tejano Alamo defenders. He saw Nava's dead body within the Alamo when authorities ordered him and other local citizens to burn the fallen defenders' corpses.*

The State of Texas, County of Béxar

Be it remembered that on this the fourth day of September A.D. 1856, before me the undersigned authority [notary public C. E. Jefferson] personally appeared Damasio de los Reyes and made oath that he was acquainted with Andrés Nava in his lifetime, that he knew him well in the years 1835 and 1836. That he was serving as a soldier with the Americans under Travis in the Alamo in February and March A.D. 1836 and was killed in the Alamo at the taking of the Alamo by Santa Anna, when Travis and Bowie and their men were massacred.

Shortly after the battle deponent with Agustín Barrera and others went into the Alamo and saw the dead body of said Nava. Deponent says that he, deponent, with others, were ordered by the authorities to go into the Alamo and gather up the dead bodies and burn them. The dead body of Nava was burned with the Americans.

Deponent says that there were seven Mexicans who fought on the side of the Americans who were killed in the Alamo, when Travis and Bowie were killed, and Andrés Nava was one of them.

- 10 -
Juana Navarro Alsbury
    Petition
    1 NOVEMBER 1857

*Juana Navarro Alsbury, who was within the Alamo when it fell, requested government compensation for the nursing services she provided during the siege and for personal property confiscated by the Mexican army after the battle.*

The State of Texas, County of Béxar
San Antonio—November 1, 1857

To the honorable the Senate and House of Representatives of the State of Texas.

The petition of Juana Navarro Alsbury respectfully referents that during the war with Mexico she was in the Alamo at the time of its fall. She was then the wife of Dr. [Horatio] Alexander Alsbury, who was taken prisoner on the 11th day of September 1842 and carried into captivity by General Adrian Woll. That during the siege of the Alamo she was ever ready to render and did render all the service she could towards nursing and attending upon the sick and wounded during said siege, which lasted some twelve or fourteen days. At the time when the place was stormed and carried by the enemy she and an only sister and a Mrs. [Susanna] Dickinson were the only females in the garrison. That all the property she had to wit her clothing, money, and jewels were seized and taken by the enemy . . . [the petitioner] prays the honorable Legislature will take her case into consideration and in view of all the circumstances allow her some compensation.

- 11 -
Francisco Esparza
Deposition
26 AUGUST 1859

*Francisco Esparza filed a deposition to support the land grant petition of his brother Gregorio's heirs. Esparza testified that his brother died defending the Alamo. He also stated that Mexican general Martín Cos granted him permission to bury Gregorio's body, probably because Francisco had fought in the Mexican army during the Texan siege of San Antonio three months earlier.*

The State of Texas, County of Béxar

Before me, Samuel S. Smith, Clerk of the County Court of Béxar County personally appeared Francisco Esparza, a citizen of Béxar County to me personally known who, being by me first duly sworn upon his oath, saith that the late Gregorio Esparza was his brother; that said Gregorio Esparza about the middle of October 1835 entered the Texas service as a volunteer and as such volunteer soldier he entered Béxar between the mornings of the 5th and 10th of December 1835 with the American forces; he remained in Béxar until the approach of General Santa Anna when he entered the Alamo [where] he was killed with Colonels Travis, Crockett, Bowie and the other Americans.

After the fall of the Alamo I applied and obtained permission from General Cos to take the body of my brother (Gregorio Esparza) and bury it. I proceeded to the Alamo and found the dead body of my brother in one of the rooms of the Alamo, he had received a ball in his breast and a stab from a sword in his side. I, in company with two of my brothers, took his body and we proceeded and interred it [in] the burying ground (*campo santo*) on the west side of the San Pedro Creek, where it still lies. My brother at the taking of Béxar was under the command of Colonel Juan N. Seguín and Captain Don Manuel Flores and a member of their company. I was in service at the time of the storming of Béxar. The company to which I belonged, the local Presidial Company of Béxar, and the soldiers of the company of the Alamo were under the capitulation of General Cos [and were] allowed to remain in Béxar with their families. I remained with my family, as I was born here and had always lived here. When Santa Anna arrived here in February 1836, he gave orders that all those who were the local soldiers at the capitulation of General Cos should hold themselves in readiness to join the army for active service, but he never called us away from our homes. I remained here when Santa Anna's army went into the interior of Texas and I am now fifty-four years of age and have lived here ever since and done and performed all the duties of a good citizen, as all my neighbors can testify. I mention these facts to show the reason why permission was given me to bury the body of my brother.

Candelario Villanueva
  Deposition
  26 AUGUST 1859

*Texas veteran Candelario Villanueva filed a deposition to support the land grant petition of Gregorio Esparza's heirs (see also document 11). Villanueva remained in the town of San Antonio during the Alamo battle and testified that afterward he entered the fortress and saw the dead bodies of Esparza, Antonio Fuentes, Toribio Losoya, Guadalupe Rodríguez, and several other Tejano defenders. He also described the circumstances which prevented him from joining his comrades during the siege.*

The State of Texas, County of Béxar

Before me, Samuel S. Smith, Clerk of the County Court of said county, personally appeared Candelario Villanueva, a citizen of Béxar County to me personally known, who being by me first duly sworn upon his oath saith that he was a member of Captain Juan N. Seguín's Company in 1835 and 1836. That he entered Béxar between the mornings of the 5th and 10th of December 1835 with the American forces; that the late Gregorio Esparza was also a soldier of Captain Juan N. Seguín's Company and he did enter Béxar with the American forces and actually assisted in the reduction of Béxar and that he remained therein till after the capitulation of General [Martín] Cos. Subsequently after the storming of Béxar the said Gregorio Esparza remained at Béxar until the approach of Santa Anna's army when he went into the Alamo with the Americans.

I remained at Béxar and when Santa Anna's troops were entering the town I started with Colonel Seguín for the Alamo, when we were on the way Colonel Seguín sent me back to lock his house up; whilst performing that duty Santa Anna's soldiers got between me and the Alamo and I had to remain in the town during the siege and assault of the Alamo. After the fall of the Alamo I went there and among the dead bodies of those lying inside of the rooms I recognized the body of Gregorio Esparza; I also saw the dead bodies of Antonio Fuentes, Toribio Losoya, Guadalupe Rodríguez and other Mexicans who had fallen in the defense of the Alamo, as also the bodies of Colonel Travis, Bowie, Crockett and other Americans that I had previously known. I saw Francisco Esparza and his brothers take the body of Gregorio Esparza and carry it off towards the *campo santo* [cemetery] for interment; the bodies of the Americans were laid in a pile and burnt. I remained in Béxar until the return of Captain Seguín and his companions after the battle of San Jacinto when I rejoined his company.

- 13 -
Brigidio Guerrero
Petition
4 JANUARY 1861

*Brigidio Guerrero requested a land grant available to Texas residents who did not abet the Mexican cause after the Texas Declaration of Independence. He testified that he was an Alamo defender and survived the final assault by concealing himself after the battle was lost.*

To the Honorable County Court of Béxar County

Your petitioner Brigidio Guerrero of the county of Béxar and state of Texas respectfully represents unto your honorable court that he was born in the year 1810 and is at present fifty years of age, that at the date of the [Texas] Declaration of Independence he was a resident citizen of Texas and a single man over seventeen years of age and as such justly entitled under the Constitution and laws of the Republic of Texas to a first class headright certificate for one third of a league of land which he has never received nor any part thereof. Your petitioner further represents and affirms on oath that far from leaving the country to avoid a participation in struggle, far from refusing to participate in the war, he was one of those who entered the Alamo under Colonel Travis in February 1836, that he was one of the defenders of that place, that he remained there up to the last moment and that, after the storming of the place by the Mexican army, [when] he saw that there was no hope left, he had the good fortune of saving his life by concealing himself, he and perhaps one other man an American being the only survivors of that awful butchery . . .

Petitioner since that time has always resided either in the city of San

Antonio or on the ranchos situated in the vicinity of that place and he believes that under the existing laws of the state of Texas he is justly entitled to claim against the state of Texas his aforesaid headright certificate as well for his military services. His ignorance of the English language and his rights prevented him from applying before for the same.

- 14 -
Francisco Antonio Ruiz
Deposition
16 APRIL 1861

*Francisco Antonio Ruiz, the mayor of San Antonio during the siege and fall of the Alamo, filed a deposition to support the land grant petition of Toribio Losoya's heirs. Ruiz testified that Santa Anna ordered him to burn the bodies of the Alamo defenders after the Mexican victory. While performing this task, he saw the dead body of Losoya who fell in the Alamo's defense.*

The State of Texas, County of Béxar

Before me Sam S. Smith Clerk of the County Court of said county personally appeared Don Francisco A[ntonio] Ruiz, a citizen of said county and state to me personally well known who being by me duly sworn upon his oath saith that during the siege and capture of the Alamo in February and March 1836 by General Santa Anna affiant was *alcalde* [mayor] of the city of San Antonio. That after the fall of the Alamo[,] General Santa Anna sent for affiant, Don Ramón Músquiz and others to identify the bodies of Travis, Bowie and Crockett which was done; that affiant was commanded by General Santa Anna to procure carts and men and proceed to make a funeral pile of the Texans, which order he carried out with much difficulty as there were but few male citizens remaining in the town, that in collecting the bodies of those that were killed in the Alamo, he recognized the body of Toribio Losoya, who had fallen fighting with the Americans in defense of the Alamo, that he knew said Toribio Losoya well [and] he was a native of Texas of Mexican blood.

PUBLISHED ACCOUNTS

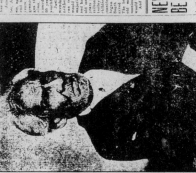

SUNDAY,     SAN ANTONIO LIGHT AND GAZETTE     APRIL 3, 1910.

# THIS MAN WAS OLD WHEN SANTA ANA SPILLED BLOOD IN ALAMO AND BUILT TEXANS' FUNERAL PYRE

## JUAN VARGAS OF SAN ANTONIO CARRIES WEIGHT OF 114 YEARS

### REMEMBERS WELL DESPERATE CHARGE AGAINST THE ALAMO

#### BY LOUIS DE NETTE

Born January 1, 1796, twenty years after American revolution, he has seen and participated in more historical events than any man alive—fought in 1810 for Mexican independence and in 1830 came to San Antonio to make his home. Five generations of the Vargas family are today alive, the youngest being Rosa, his 3-year-old great - great - grandchild. His life and experiences related by himself.

W HERE is the man who, having stepped past the Biblical three score and ten milestone, believes he is old? Where is the man who, as he nears the century mark, feels the weight of his years and believes that indeed he is aged in the land?

All honor to them! They, in their own and other's estimation, are old. They may contemplate the past from the lapse of time. But here in San Antonio is a man on whose head rests the ac-

Vargas Is a Pure Blood Aztec Indian of the Tribe of President Diaz of Mexico. He Was Born in Oaxaca, Mexico, in 1796, and Is Over 114 Years Old. He Claims to San Antonio 70 Years Ago.

### NEW CHURCH TO AMERICANS WILL BE CONSECRATED RULE ISLANDS

Lutheran Edifice on Mount of Holy    See Will at Once Appoint
Olives to Be Dedicated     Bishops From the Ranks
By the Germans.      of the Church Here.

## - 15 -

## Juan N. Seguín

*Personal Memoirs of John N. Seguín*

1858

*Texas veteran Juan Nepomuceno Seguín left his native San Antonio in 1842 under threat of Anglo-American persecution. He returned after the Mexican War and published his* Memoirs *to vindicate his name. In these* Memoirs *Seguín recounted his distinguished military service to the Republic of Texas, including his escape as a courier from the besieged Alamo and his futile efforts to enlist the support of Colonel James Walker Fannin and his troops.*

On the 22nd of February at two o'clock P.M., General Santa Anna took possession of the city [San Antonio] with over four thousand men and in the meantime we fell back on the Alamo.

On the 28th, the enemy commenced the bombardment, meanwhile we met in a Council of War and, taking into consideration our perilous situation, it was resolved by a majority of the council that I should leave the fort and proceed with a communication to Colonel Fannin, requesting him to come to our assistance. I left the Alamo on the night of the council; on the following day I met, at the Ranch of San Bartolo on the Cibolo, Captain [Francis L.] Desauque who, by orders of Fannin, had foraged on my ranch, carrying off a great number of beeves, corn, etc. Desauque informed me that Fannin could not delay more than two days his arrival at the Cibolo, on his way to render assistance to the defenders of the Alamo. I therefore determined to wait for him. I sent Fannin, by express, the communication from Travis, informing him at the same time of the critical position of the defenders of the Alamo. Fannin answered me, through Lieutenant [Charles] Finley, that he had advanced as far as Rancho Nuevo but, being informed of the movements of General [José] Urrea, he had countermarched to Goliad to defend that place; adding that he could not respond to Travis' call, their respective commands being separate and depending upon General Houston, then at Gonzales, with whom he advised me to communicate. I lost no time in repairing to Gonzales and reported myself to the General, informing him of the purpose of my mission. He commanded me to wait at Gonzales for further orders . . .

On the 6th of March, I received orders to go to San Antonio with my company and a party of American citizens, carrying on the horses provisions for the defenders of the Alamo.

Arrived at the Cibolo and, not hearing the signal gun which was to be discharged every fifteen minutes as long as the place held out, we retraced our steps to convey to the General-in-Chief the sad tidings. A new party was sent out, which soon came back, having met with Anselmo Bergara and Andrés Barcena, both soldiers of my company, whom I had left for purposes of observation in the vicinity of San Antonio; they brought the intelligence of the fall of the Alamo. Their report was so circumstantial as to preclude any doubts about that disastrous event.

*Francisco Antonio Ruiz.*
*Courtesy Mr. Adolfo C. Herrera,*
*San Antonio. Photograph on file*
*at Institute of Texan Cultures,*
*San Antonio.*

- 16 -
Francisco Antonio Ruiz
    *The Texas Almanac for 1860*

*Francisco Antonio Ruiz, the mayor of San Antonio during the siege and fall of the Alamo, provided the first published Tejano account of the battle itself. Ruiz witnessed the siege and battle from the town of San Antonio. Afterward Santa Anna ordered him to enter the walls of the fortress and oversee the disposal of corpses. José Agustín Quintero, a Cuban emigrant and former editor of the* San Antonio Ranchero, *translated the Ruiz account.*

## FALL OF THE ALAMO, AND MASSACRE OF TRAVIS AND HIS BRAVE ASSOCIATES

by Francis Antonio Ruiz—Translated by J. A. Quintero

On the 23rd day of February 1836 (two o'clock P.M.), General Santa Anna entered the city of San Antonio with a part of his army. This he effected without any resistance, the forces under the command of Travis, Bowie, and Crockett having on the same day, at eight o'clock in the morning, learned that the Mexican army was on the banks of the Medina River, they concentrated in the fortress of the Alamo.

In the evening they commenced to exchange fire with guns and from the 23rd of February to the 6th of March (in which the storming was made by Santa Anna) the roar of artillery and volleys of musketry were constantly heard.

On the 6th of March, at three o'clock P.M., General Santa Anna at the head of four thousand men advanced against the Alamo. The infantry, artillery, and cavalry had formed about one thousand varas from the walls of said fortress. The Mexican army charged and were twice repulsed by the deadly fire of Travis' artillery, which resembled a constant thunder. At the third charge the Toluca battalion commenced to scale the walls and suffered severely. Out of eight hundred men, 130 were only left alive.

When the Mexican army had succeeded in entering the walls I, with the Political Chief (*jefe político*), Don Ramón Músquiz, and other members of the Corporation accompanied the Curate, Don Refugio de la Garza who, by Santa Anna's orders, had assembled during the night at a temporary fortification erected in Potrero Street, with the object of attending the wounded, etc. As soon as the storming commenced, we crossed the bridge on Commerce Street with this object in view and about one hundred yards from the same a party of Mexican dragoons fired upon us and compelled us to fall back on the river and place we occupied before. Half an hour had elapsed when Santa Anna sent one of his aids-de-camp with an order for us to come before him. He directed me to call on some of the neighbors to come up with carts to carry the dead to the cemetery and also to accompany him, as he was desirous to have Colonels Travis, Bowie, and Crockett shown to him.

On the north battery of the fortress lay the lifeless body of Colonel Travis on the gun carriage, *shot* only in the forehead. Toward the west and in the small fort opposite the city, we found the body of Colonel Crockett. Colonel Bowie was found dead in his bed, in one of the rooms of the south side.

Santa Anna, after all the Mexicans were taken out, ordered wood to be brought to burn the bodies of the Texians. He sent a company of dragoons with me to bring wood and dry branches from the neighboring forest. About three o'clock in the afternoon they commenced laying the wood and dry branches, upon which a file of dead bodies was placed; more wood was piled on them and another file brought and in this manner they were all arranged in layers. Kindling wood was distributed through the pile and about five o'clock in the evening it was lighted.

The dead Mexicans of Santa Anna were taken to the graveyard but, not having sufficient room for them, I ordered some of them to be thrown in the river, which was done on the same day.

Santa Anna's loss was estimated at sixteen hundred men. These were the flower of his army.

The gallantry of the few Texians who defended the Alamo was really wondered at by the Mexican army. Even the generals were astonished at their vigorous resistance and how dearly victory had been bought.

The generals who, under Santa Anna, participated in the storming of the Alamo were Juan [Valentín] Amador, [Manuel Fernández] Castrillón, [Joaquín] Ramírez [y] Sesma, and [Juan José] Andrade.

The men burnt numbered 182. I was an eyewitness, for as *alcalde* [mayor] of San Antonio I was with some of the neighbors collecting the dead bodies and placing them on the funeral pyre.

Signed, Francisco Antonio Ruiz

P.S. My father was Don Francisco Ruiz, a member of the Texas Convention. He signed the Declaration of Independence on the 2nd day of March, 1836.

Juana Navarro Alsbury
   John S. Ford Memoirs
   c. 1880s

*John Salmon Ford, a renowned Texas veteran, political figure, and history enthusiast, procured Juana Navarro Alsbury's testimony as a source for his writings on the Alamo battle. Recorded some fifty years after the battle, this vivid account is one of the few sources attributed to adults who survived the final assault on the Alamo. Although previously unpublished, Navarro Alsbury's account is included in this section because, like many published accounts of this period, it is a relatively extensive narrative obtained by an interviewer.*

   Mrs. Alsbury's Recollections of the Alamo

Juana, the daughter of Angel Navarro and a niece of Colonel José Antonio Navarro, when very young was adopted by Governor [Juan Martín] Veramendi, who had married her father's sister. Señorita Juana married a Mexican gentleman, Don Alejo Pérez, by whom she had a son, Alejo, who is a respectable citizen of San Antonio. The elder Pérez died in 1834 and his widow married Dr. Horatio Alexander Alsbury early in 1836. It must be remembered that Colonel James Bowie married the daughter of Governor Veramendi, consequently his wife was the cousin and the adopted sister of Mrs. Alsbury. This accounts for her being in his charge and in the Alamo.

   When the news of Santa Anna's approach at the head of a considerable force was verified in San Antonio, Dr. Alsbury proceeded to the Brazos River to procure means to remove his family, expecting to return before Santa Anna could reach the city. He failed to do so; and his wife went into the Alamo where her protector was, when the Mexican troops were near by. She was accompanied by her younger sister, Gertrudis. Colonel Bowie was very sick of typhoid fever. For that reason he thought it prudent to be removed from the part of the buildings occupied by Mrs. Alsbury. A couple of soldiers carried him away. On leaving he said: "Sister, do not be afraid. I leave you with Colonel Travis, Colonel Crockett, and other friends. They are gentlemen and will treat you kindly." He had himself brought back two or three times to see and talk with her. Their last interview took place three or four days before the fall of the Alamo. She never saw him again, either alive or dead.

She says she does not know who nursed him after he left the quarters she occupied and expresses no disbelief in the statement of Madam Candelaria [Andrea Castañón Villanueva]. "There were people in the Alamo I did not see."

Mrs. Alsbury and her sister were in a building not far from where the residence of Colonel Sam Maverick was afterwards erected. It was considered quite a safe locality. They saw very little of the fighting. While the final struggle was progressing she peeped out and saw the surging columns of Santa Anna assaulting the Alamo on every side, as she believed. She could hear the noise of the conflict—the roar of the artillery, the rattle of the small arms, the shouts of the combatants, the groans of the dying, and the moans of the wounded. The firing approximated where she was and she realized the fact that the brave Texians had been overwhelmed by numbers. She asked her sister to go to the door and request the Mexican soldiers not to fire into the room, as it contained women only. Señorita Gertrudis opened the door, she was greeted in offensive language by the soldiers. Her shawl was torn from her shoulders and she rushed back into the room. During this period Mrs. Alsbury was standing with her one-year-old son strained to her bosom, supposing he would be motherless soon. The soldiers then demanded of Señorita Gertrudis: "Your money and your husband." She replied: "I have neither money nor husband." About this time a sick man ran up to Mrs. Alsbury and attempted to protect her. The soldiers bayoneted him at her side. She thinks his name was Mitchell.

After this tragic event a young Mexican, hotly pursued by soldiers, seized her by the arm and endeavored to keep her between himself and his assailants. His grasp was broken and four or five bayonets plunged into his body and nearly as many balls went through his lifeless corpse. The soldiers broke open her trunk and took her money and clothes, also the watch of Colonel Travis and other officers.

A Mexican officer appeared on the scene. He excitedly inquired, "How did you come here? What are you doing here any how? Where is the entrance to the fort?" He made her pass out of the room over a cannon standing nearby the door. He told her to remain there and he would have her sent to President Santa Anna. Another officer came up and asked: "What

*El Dia 23 de Julio de 1888*
*fallecio a las 4 ½ de la tarde*
*a la edad de 78 años en*
*el Rancho de la Laguna*
*redonda donde esta*
*Sepultada.*
                    *Alejo E. Perez*

Death Notice of Juana Navarro Alsbury. The inscription states that she died at 4:30 P.M. on 23 July 1888 at the age of 78. She died at the Laguna Ranch and was buried nearby. This notice is in the personal journal of Juana's son, Alejo E. Pérez, and is written in his hand. Pérez was the last survivor of the Alamo battle at the time of his death in 1918. Courtesy Dorothy Marie Pérez. Photograph from original taken by staff at Institute of Texan Cultures, San Antonio.

Gertrudis Navarro Cantú, sister of Juana Navarro Alsbury and survivor of the Alamo battle. CN08198, Gertrudis Navarro file, Prints and Photographs Collection, Center for American History, University of Texas, Austin.

are you doing here?" She replied: "An officer ordered us to remain here and he would have us sent to the President." "President the devil. Don't you see they are about to fire that cannon? Leave." They were moving when they heard a voice calling "Sister." "To my great relief Don Manuel Pérez came to us. He said: 'Don't you know your own brother-in-law?' I answered: 'I am so excited and distressed that I scarcely know anything.'" Don Manuel placed them in charge of a colored woman belonging to Colonel Bowie and the party reached the house of Don Angel Navarro in safety.

Mrs. Alsbury says to the best of her remembrance she heard firing at the Alamo till twelve o'clock that day.

She says the name of the girl Santa Anna deceived by false marriage was [left blank].

She describes Colonel Bowie as a tall, well made gentleman, of a very serious countenance, of few words, always to the point, and a warm friend. In his family he was affectionate, kind, and so acted as to secure the love and confidence of all.


- 18 -

Juan N. Seguín
   *Clarksville Standard*
   4 MARCH 1887

*This interview of the aging Juan Nepomuceno Seguín expands on an earlier account in his* Memoirs *(see document 15) by describing the danger entailed in his departure as a courier from the beleaguered Alamo.*

Colonel Juan N. Seguín

A representative of the [*Laredo*] *Times* called on the venerable Colonel Juan N. Seguín, sole surviving captain of the Texan army participating in the battle of San Jacinto. Colonel Seguín was born in San Antonio, October 29th [27th], 1806, and is consequently eighty years of age. He comes of pure Castilian descent, his ancestors being of the first colony that came from the Canaries to San Fernando, as San Antonio was first called. He would easily pass now for a man of sixty, so gently has time indented its furrows upon his brow and face, although his hair is snow white. In personal appearance Colonel Seguín is about five feet eight inches tall and rather heavy, doubtless weighing 170 or 180 pounds. His complexion is fair, his features regular, and the general expression of the countenance indicating firmness and gentleness of heart. As a commander his force must have lain rather in persuasion and the love of his men, than in the exercise of stern power, as was largely the case with General [Lawrence Sullivan?] Ross. His manner is dignified yet kindly and confidential, and tears came to his eyes as he dwelt upon the stirring scenes of 1836 and he inquired of his friends of that period and of their descendants. Of those known to the writer, only one survives: Mr. Thomas O'Connor, of Refugio; and as the old veteran inquired of John J. Linn, Edward Linn, John S. Menefee, and others, the answer was "Dead!" In many respects Colonel Seguín was a unique figure in the Texas Revolution, siding as he did against the majority of his countrymen. That he was actuated by the purest of patriotic motives there can be no doubt, and equally as true is it that he contributed his full share in achieving the independence of Texas. He was shut up in the Alamo by the encircling lines of Santa Anna's army and was the fourth and last messenger sent out by Travis for aid, Major Red [John W. "Red" Smith?] being the only one so sent whose name he could recall. The message was verbal, directing Colonel [James Walker] Fannin, at La Bahía (Goliad) to march to his rescue. His egress from the beleaguered Alamo was under the friendly cover of darkness and was attended with great danger, as the fort was entirely surrounded and bombs were bursting all around. He, however, stealthily made his way through the Mexican lines on foot and often upon all fours. A horse was procured at a ranch and he rode night and day until La Bahía was reached and faithfully delivered the message to Colonel Fannin. Colonel Seguín says Fannin said it would be impossible for him to comply, as General [José] Urrea was then near his position. Being unable to re-enter the Alamo, and fortunately for him, Colonel Seguín went to Gonzales, at which point was General Houston and the Texan army. Here he organized his company, a brave and gallant band of Mexicans who did their whole duty at San Jacinto.

Juan N. Seguín
  Letter to William Winston Fontaine
  7 JUNE 1890

*Written less than three months before his death, this letter is the final recorded
Alamo recollection of Tejano veteran Juan Nepomuceno Seguín. In two earlier
accounts Seguín described his role as a courier for the Alamo garrison (see
documents 15 and 18). This narration adds further details about the siege of
the Alamo before his departure.*

Your favor of the 26th May ultimate to hand and contents carefully noted.
In answer, I beg to state, that I am glad to be able to be of service to you in
the recollection of those days of glory long past, but not forgotten. Santa
Anna's army was drawn up before Béxar on the 22nd day of February 1836.

Colonel Travis had no idea that Santa Anna with his army would venture to approach the city of Béxar (now San Antonio) and for this reason
only a watch was kept on the church tower that existed where today stands
the cathedral of San Fernando; this watchman was an American whose
name I do not now remember. About three o'clock in the afternoon he
sent a messenger stating that on the road to León he saw a moving body
which appeared like a line of troops raising the dust of the road. Upon the
receipt of this notice John W. Smith, a carpenter (alias "el colorado"), was
sent to reconnoiter and returned in the evening about five o'clock saying
"there comes the Mexican army composed of cavalry, infantry and artillery!" In the act of the moment Colonel Travis resolved to concentrate all
his forces within the Alamo, which was immediately done. As we marched
"Potrero Street" (now called "Commerce") the ladies exclaimed, "Poor fel-
lows, you will all be killed, what shall we do?"

Santa Anna occupied the city of Béxar at about seven o'clock in the
afternoon of that same day and immediately established the siege of the
Alamo, which at first was not rigorously kept as the sons of a widow named
Pacheco, one of whom was named Estéban, took me my meals, and by
them we were enabled to communicate with those external to the Alamo.

The day following the arrival of Santa Anna the bombardment was vig-
orously commenced and lasted three days. Finding ourselves in such a desperate situation, Colonel Travis resolved to name a messenger to proceed

to the town of Gonzales and ask for help—thinking that Sam Houston was then at that place. But, as to leave the fortification at such a critical moment was the same as to encounter death, Santa Anna having now drawn as it were a complete circle of iron around the Alamo, no one would consent to run the risk, making it necessary to decide the question by putting it to a vote; I was the one elected. Colonel Travis opposed my taking this commission, stating that as I was the only one that possessed the Spanish language and understood Mexican customs better, my presence in the Alamo might become necessary in case of having to treat with Santa Anna. But the rest could not be persuaded and I must go. I was permitted to take my orderly Antonio Cruz [Arocha] and we left [at] eight o'clock at night after having bid good bye to all my comrades, expecting certain death. I arrived safely at the town of Gonzales and obtained at once a reinforcement of thirty men, who were sent to the Alamo, and I proceeded to meet Sam Houston.

When the notice of the arrival of the thirty men was given to Santa Anna, it is said, he gave orders to allow them entrance stating that he would only have that many more to kill.

In the city of Béxar at the time of which we speak there were no others by the name of Seguín than my father Don Erasmo Seguín and myself. My father was then judge of the Probate Court and I was commander of the Fourth Department of the West, with headquarters in Béxar.

Even though there may have been a misunderstanding between Bowie and my father, the forces of Colonel Travis did not reach the Medina then.

Colonel [James Butler] Bonham was about six feet in height, thin, fair complexion, brown hair, gray eyes, he was not vicious and of very honorable conduct as I knew.

- 20 -

Andrea Castañón Villanueva
*San Antonio Express*
6 MARCH 1892

*Visitors to San Antonio frequently interviewed Andrea Castañón Villanueva, more popularly known as Madam Candelaria, as a survivor of the Alamo battle. Madam Candelaria was the wife of Candelario Villanueva (see document 12). Although other witnesses contest her presence within the Alamo during the battle, she received government compensation for services which included assistance during the siege and final assault. Like other accounts of the aging Candelaria, this testimony is based on an interview conducted in Spanish.*

*Andrea Castañón Villanueva, more commonly known as Madam Candelaria. CN08089, Madam Candelaria file, Prints and Photographs Collection, Center for American History, University of Texas, Austin.*

## FALL OF THE ALAMO
*Historical Reminiscences of the Aged Madam Candelaria*
Her Statement as to the Manner of Bowie's Death Differs from That in Histories—An Anniversary Event

The name of Madam Candelaria is a household word in San Antonio. She is without doubt the oldest living native of Texas, being 107 [88] years of age as is shown by the certificate of the priest who administered to her spiritual wants in her childhood. This certificate is in Spanish and its authenticity cannot be disputed. The aged heroine lives in a typical Mexican house on South Laredo Street, where she is visited by hundreds of tourists and old friends in the course of a year. On this day, the anniversary of the fall of the Alamo, it is befitting that a sketch of Madam Candelaria, who was in the midst of that stirring historical affair, be given. In order to secure a statement from her own lips a reporter for the *Express* in company with an interpreter visited her yesterday.

When the unpretentious dwelling of the centenarian [*sic*] was entered she rose from her comfortable chair and extended a cordial greeting to the visitors. The more than one hundred years [*sic*] that have passed over her head have not affected her voice in the least and she speaks the soft, musical Spanish language with a force and warmth that is entertaining and faultless in expression. In response to an inquiry of the reporter she stated that she was born on November 30, 1785 [1803] at Laredo, Texas and the priest's certificate bears out her statement.

"My father said he was the tailor of Ferdinand VII and after my birth I lived several years at Laredo with my parents. There were only a few houses there at that time and they were mere *jacales* [huts] covered with hides. I was first taken by my father to Rio Grande City and then to Zaragosa. After living there a few years I lived in various places in what is now the state of Coahuila, but which was at that time embraced in the state of Texas. I afterward lived in Nacogdoches and in 1820 came to San Antonio. This was a mere village at that time and was occupied by General [Anastacio?] Bustamante and his troops."

In relating her reminiscences of the fall of the Alamo Madam Candelaria stated that she was called upon a few days before the fatal attack was made [in order] to nurse Colonel Bowie, who was very sick of typhoid fever.

"Santa Anna made the attack," she continued, "on March 6. The Alamo was filled with Texans, a number of women being among them. Colonel Bowie died in my arms only a few minutes before the entrance to the Alamo by the soldiers. I was holding his head in my lap when Santa Anna's men swarmed into the room where I was sitting. One of them thrust a bayonet into the lifeless head of Colonel Bowie and lifted his body from my lap. As he did so the point of the weapon slipped and struck me in the jaw," and here the aged heroine showed the scar of the wound which she had received.

During her recital of this exciting experience she made numerous expressive gesticulations, swaying her body to and fro in a highly dramatic style.

- 21 -

Eulalia Yorba
*San Antonio Express*
12 APRIL 1896

*In an interview conducted well after her ninetieth birthday, Eulalia Yorba recalled her experiences in the town of San Antonio during the siege of the*

*Alamo, as well as her observation, from a distance, of the final assault. Yorba attended the wounded Mexican soldiers within the Alamo after it fell; her account includes her poignant memories of the battle's aftermath.*

## ANOTHER STORY OF THE ALAMO
*The Battle Described by an Alleged Eye Witness*
How Santa Anna's Overwhelming Forces Attacked and Captured
the Enemy's Stronghold—The Death of Davy Crockett

There is now living in the United States but one person who saw the awful conflict. She is Señora Eulalia Yorba, a poor old Spanish woman, who lives in the suburbs at Fort Worth. She was born in 1801 and is therefore nearly ninety-five years of age. She was thirty-four when the Alamo was besieged. She lives with her granddaughter's family and is supplied with a little means of livelihood by the well-to-do citizens of San Antonio and Fort Worth, who take just pride in the memories of the old Spanish woman of the battle at the stone mission. Her mind is very keen on events of sixty and seventy years ago and she has been sought after by numerous writers of history in the Southwest.

The writer had a most interesting interview with Mrs. Yorba not long ago and communicated the results to the *San Francisco Examiner.* Everyone in Fort Worth knows where to find her and we were soon at her door. She said:

I well remember when Santa Anna and his two thousand soldiers on horses and with shining muskets and bayonets marched into the little pueblo of San Antonio. The news ran from mouth to mouth that Colonel Travis, Davy Crockett and Colonel Bowie and the 160 or so other Texans who had held that locality against the Mexicans for several weeks had taken refuge in and had barricaded themselves in that old stone mission, which had been used as a crude fort or garrison long before I came to the country. It belonged to Mexico and a few stands of muskets and three or four cannons were kept there. When Santa Anna's army came they camped on the plains about the pueblo and a guard was put about the Alamo fort. That was from the last day of February to March 4. Of course, I kept at home with my little boys and never stirred out once, for we women were all terribly frightened. Every eatable in the house, all the cows, lumber and hay about the place were taken by the troops, but we were assured that if we remained in the house no personal harm would come to us.

Of course, we were hourly informed of the news. We knew that the Texans in the Alamo were surrounded by over five hundred soldiers constantly, while fifteen hundred more soldiers were in camp out on the plains. We learned that four days had been given the Texans to surrender. We heard from the soldiers that not one of the imprisoned men had so much as returned a reply to the demand for surrender and that on the morning of the 6th of March 1836, Santa Anna was going to bring matters to a crisis with the beleaguered rebels. I never can tell the anxiety that we people on the outside felt for that mere handful of men in the old fort, when we saw around hostile troops as far as we could see and not a particle of help for the Texans, for whom we few residents of the town had previously formed a liking.

The morning of Sunday—the 6th of March—ah! indeed, I could never forget that, even if I lived many years more—was clear and balmy and every scrap of food was gone from my house and the children and I ran to the home of a good old Spanish priest so that we could have food and comfort there. There was nothing to impede the view of the Alamo from the priest's home, although I wished there was. The shooting began at six in the morning. It seemed as if there were myriads of soldiers and guns about the stone building. There was volley after volley fired into the barred and bolted windows. Then the volleys came in quick succession. Occasionally we heard muffled volleys and saw puffs of smoke from within the Alamo, and when we saw, too, Mexican soldiers fall in the roadway or stagger back we knew the Texans were fighting as best they could for their lives.

It seemed as if ten thousand guns were shot off indiscriminately as firecrackers snap when whole bundles of them are set off at one time. The smoke grew thick and heavy and we could not see clearly down at the Alamo, while the din of musketry, screams of crazy, exultant Mexicans increased every moment. I have never heard human beings scream so fiercely and powerfully as the Mexican soldiers that day. I can compare such screams only to the yell of a mountain panther or lynx in desperate straits.

Next several companies of soldiers came running down the street with great heavy bridge timbers. These were quickly brought to bear as battering rams on the mission doors, but several volleys from within the Alamo, as nearly as we could see, laid low the men at the timbers and stopped the battering for a short time. Three or four brass cannons were loaded with what seemed to us very long delay and were placed directly in front of the main doors of the mission. They did serious work. Meanwhile, bullets from several thousand muskets incessantly rained like hail upon the building and went through the apertures that had been made in the wood barricades at the windows and doors. The din was indescribable. It did not seem as if a mouse could live in a building so shot at and riddled as the Alamo was that morning.

Next we saw ladders brought and in a trice the low roof of the church was crowded with a screaming, maddened throng of men armed with guns and sabers. Of course we knew then that it was all up with the little band of men in the Alamo. I remember that the priest drew us away from the window and refused to let us look longer, notwithstanding the fascination of the scene. We could still hear the shouts and yells and the booming of the brass cannon shook the priest's house and rattled the window panes.

Along about nine o'clock, I should judge, the shooting and swearing and yelling had ceased, but the air was thick and heavy with blue powder smoke. A Mexican colonel came running to the priest's residence and asked that we go down to the Alamo to do what we could for the dying men.

Such a dreadful sight. The roadway was thronged with Mexican soldiers with smoke and dirt begrimed faces, haggard eyes and wild, insane expression. There were twelve or fifteen bodies of Mexicans lying dead and bleeding here and there and others were being carried to an adobe house across the way. The stones in the church wall were spotted with blood, the doors were splintered and battered in. Pools of thick blood were so frequent on the sun-baked earth about the stone building that we had to be careful to avoid stepping in them. There was a din of excited voices along the street and the officers were marshaling their men for moving to camp.

But no one could even tell you the horror of the scene that met our gaze when we were led by the sympathetic little colonel into the old Alamo to bandage up the wounds of several young men there. I used to try when I was younger to describe that awful sight, but I never could find sufficient language. There were only a few Mexicans in there when we came and they were all officers who had ordered the common soldiers away from the scene of death and—yes—slaughter, for that was what it was. The floor was literally crimson with blood. The woodwork all about us was riddled and splintered by lead balls and what was left of the old altar at the rear of the church was cut and slashed by cannon ball and bullets. The air was dark with powder smoke and was hot and heavy. The odor was oppressive and sickening and the simply horrible scene nerved us as nothing else could.

The dead Texans lay singly and in heaps of three or four, or in irregular rows here and there all about the floor of the Alamo, just as they had fallen when a ball reached a vital part or they had dropped to their death from loss of blood. Of course we went to work as soon as we got to the mission at helping the bleeding and moaning men, who had only a few hours at most more of life; but the few minutes that we looked upon the corpses all about us gave a picture that has always been as distinct as one before my very eyes.

So thick were the bodies of the dead that we had to step over them to get [near] a man in whom there was still life. Close to my feet was a young man who had been shot through the forehead. He had dropped dead with his eyes staring wildly open and, as he lay there, seemingly gazed up into my face.

I remember seeing poor old Colonel Davy Crockett as he lay dead by the side of a dying man, whose bloody and powder-stained face I was washing. Colonel Crockett was about fifty years old at that time. His coat and rough woolen shirt were soaked with blood so that the original color was hidden, for the eccentric hero must have died of some ball in the chest or a bayonet thrust.

- 22 -

Andrea Castañón Villanueva
*San Antonio Light*
19 FEBRUARY 1899

*Shortly after Andrea Castañón Villanueva's death at San Antonio, a local newspaper republished this earlier account of hers from the* St. Louis Republic. *The woman more commonly known as Madam Candelaria was frequently interviewed as a survivor of the Alamo battle (see document 20); these reminiscences are her most vivid narration of the final assault.*

ALAMO MASSACRE
*As Told by the Late Madam Candelaria*
Her Vivid Story of the Great Battle, Where 177 Brave Men
Met Death as True Heroes—Colonel Bowie Died in Her Arms—
Blood Was Ankle Deep

The *St. Louis Republic* recently published a lengthy article about the late Madam Candelaria and the battle of the Alamo which will prove of interest to San Antonians:

Old Madam Candelaria says that she has heard and read a hundred different descriptions of the battle of the Alamo and that not one is correct. Although she is now in her one hundred and sixteenth [95th] year, her health is good and her mind is perfectly clear as to events that transpired in the early part of the century. Her great age and the conspicuous and heroic part that she enacted during the famous siege of the Alamo are matters that are well authentic[ated] and beyond all question of doubt. A few years ago the Texas Legislature appointed a committee to wait upon this very remarkable woman and investigate all the facts connected with her claims upon the gratitude of the state. After examining many witnesses and looking over the records preserved in the old missions, they reported that no doubt could exist as to the fact that Madam Candelaria was inside of the walls of the Alamo engaged in nursing Colonel James Bowie at the time the battle was fought and further declared that they believed she was born in the year A.D. 1782 [1803]. Acting upon this report and prompted by a commendable desire to promptly recognize and reward the services of one who had done so much to aid in the establishment of the old republic, the legislature granted a pension of one hundred dollars a year to this heroic old wlady.

Madam Candelaria is still alive and living in a small adobe house at 611 Laredo Street, San Antonio. Nothing pleases her better than to receive a visitor who manifests interest in her story of the fall of the Alamo. She is totally blind and though rather feeble and somewhat slow and hesitating in the use of the English language, she manages, through rapid and emphatic gestures, occasionally assisted by a Spanish girl who is constantly by her side, to give an attentive listener a very impressive description of one of the most remarkable battles ever fought in the history of the world . . .

Though every drop of her blood is Spanish blood, she has never loved

Spain, from the fact that her father's family was forcibly moved to Texas from the Canary Islands about the middle of the last century for the purpose of carrying out a colonization scheme, concerning which her people were never consulted . . .

In 1836 she kept a hotel in San Antonio and her house was always at the disposal of Houston, Austin, Travis, Lamar and such other daring spirits as were at that time committing themselves to the cause of Texas freedom. All of the old warriors knew her well and all of them admired her many fine traits of character and her patriotic devotion to the sacred principles, for maintenance of which many of them afterwards sacrificed their lives. James Bowie had been living in San Antonio for several years, where he was very popular with all classes. The Mexicans, who were still attached to the old country, hoped that he would embrace their cause, from the fact that he had married a beautiful Mexican girl. But the alarm was no sooner sounded than this man of peerless valor offered his services to Texas. When Santa Anna suddenly appeared on the prairies, in sight of San Antonio, at the head of a veteran army of ten thousand men, Colonel Bowie was very sick. Hopeful as all are who are afflicted with consumption, he still felt himself able to discharge the duties of a soldier. He went to the Alamo and declared that he would fight as a private. It was not long before he was confined to his cot. General Houston wrote a letter to Madam Candelaria, which she still possesses, asking her to look after his friend Bowie and nurse him herself. All save Bowie himself realized that the hero was in the last stages of consumption.

When Santa Anna invested the city and drew a cordon of troops around the Alamo, Madam Candelaria was inside of the walls. She might easily have returned to her home, but her heart was with the patriots and she determined to remain with them and share their fortunes. Bowie grew worse every day. He was never able to sit up more than a few moments at any period during the time that the battle was going on. He occupied the little room on the left of the great front door and Madam Candelaria sat by his side. When the firing grew hot he would ask his faithful nurse to assist him to raise himself to the window. He would aim deliberately and after firing would fall back on his cot and rest. One evening Colonel Travis made a fine speech to his soldiers. Madam Candelaria does not pretend to remember what he said, but she does remember that he drew a line on the floor with the point of his sword and asked all who were willing to die for

Texas to come over on his side. They all quickly stepped across the line but two men. One of these sprang over the wall and disappeared. The other man was James Bowie. He made an effort to rise, but failed, and with tears streaming from his eyes he said: "Boys, won't none of you help me over there?" Colonel Davy Crockett and several others instantly sprang towards the cot and carried the brave man across the line. Madam Candelaria noticed Crockett drop on his knees and talk earnestly in low tones to Colonel Bowie for a long time. "At this time," says the heroic old lady, "we all knew that we were doomed, but not one was in favor of surrendering. A small herd of cattle had been driven inside of the walls and we had found a small quantity of corn that had been stored by the priests. The great front door had been piled full of sand bags and there was a bare hope that we might hold out until General Houston sent a reinforcement.

"There was just 177 men inside of the Alamo and up to this time no one had been killed, though cannon had thundered against us and several assaults had been made. Colonel Travis was the first man killed. He fell on the southeast side near where the Menger Hotel stands. The Mexican infantry charged across the plaza many times and rained musket balls against the walls, but they were always made to recoil. Up to the morning of the 6th of March, the cannon had done us little damage, though the batteries never ceased firing. Colonel Crockett frequently came into the room and said a few encouraging words to Bowie. This man came to San Antonio only a few days before the invasion. The Americans extended him a warm welcome. They made bonfires in the streets and Colonel Crockett must have made a great speech, for I never heard so much cheering and hurrahing in all my life. They had supper at my hotel and there was lots of singing, story telling and some drinking. Crockett played the fiddle and he played well if I am any judge of music. He was one of the strangest looking men I ever saw. He had the face of a woman and his manner was that of a young girl. I could not regard him as a hero until I saw him die. He looked grand and terrible standing in the door and fighting a whole column of Mexican infantry. He had fired his last shot and had no time to reload. The cannon balls had knocked away the sand bags and the infantry was pouring through the breech. Crockett stood there swinging something bright over his head. The place was full of smoke and I could not tell whether he was using a gun or a sword. A heap of dead was piled at his feet and the Mexicans were lunging at him with bayonets, but he would not retreat an inch. Poor

Bowie could see it all, but he could not raise up from his cot. Crockett fell and the Mexicans poured into the Alamo."

On the morning of the 6th of March 1836, General Santa Anna prepared to hurl his whole force against the doomed fort. The *degüello* [bugle call signifying no quarter] was sounded and Madam Candelaria says that they all very well understood what it meant and every man prepared to sell his life as dearly as possible.

The soldiers with blanched cheeks and a look of fearless firmness gathered in groups and conversed in low tones. Colonel Crockett and about a dozen strong men stood with their guns in their hands behind the sand bags at the front. The cot upon which Colonel Bowie reposed was in the little room on the north side, within a few feet of the position occupied by Crockett and his men. These two brave spirits frequently exchanged a few words while waiting for the Mexicans to begin the battle. "I sat by Bowie's side," says Madam Candelaria, "and tried to keep him as composed as possible. He had a high fever and was seized with a fit of coughing every few moments. Colonel Crockett loaded Bowie's rifle and a pair of pistols and laid them by his side. The Mexicans ran a battery of several guns out on the plaza and instantly began to rain balls against the sand bags. It was easy to see that they would soon clear every barricade from the front door, but Crockett assured Bowie that he could stop a whole regiment from entering. I peeped through the window and saw long lines of infantry, followed by dragoons, filing into the plaza, and I notified Colonel Crockett of the fact. 'All right,' said he. 'Boys, aim well.' The words had hardly died on his lips before a storm of bullets rained against the walls and the very earth seemed to tremble beneath the tread of Santa Anna's yelling legions. The Texans made every shot tell and the plaza was covered with dead bodies. The assaulting columns recoiled and I thought we had beaten them, but hosts of officers could be seen waving their swords and rallying the hesitating and broken columns.

"They charged again and at one time, when within a dozen steps of the door, it looked as if they were about to be driven back, so terrible was the fire of the Texans. Those immediately in front of the great door were certainly in the act of retiring when a column that had come obliquely across the plaza reached the southwest corner of the Alamo and, bending their bodies, they ran under the shelter of the wall to the door. It looked as if a hundred bayonets were thrust into the door at the same time and a sheet of flame lit up the Alamo. Every man at the door fell but Crockett. I could see him struggling with the head of the column and Bowie raised up and fired his rifle. I saw Crockett fall backwards. The enraged Mexicans then streamed into the building firing and yelling like madmen. The place was full of smoke and the death screams of the dying, mingled with the exultant shouts of the victors, made it a veritable hell. A dozen or more Mexicans sprang into the room occupied by Colonel Bowie. He emptied his pistols in their faces and killed two of them. As they lunged towards him with their muskets I threw myself in front of them and received two of their bayonets in my body. One passed through my arm and the other through the flesh of my chin. Here, Señor, are the scars; you can see them yet. I implored them not to murder a sick man, but they thrust me out of the way and butchered my friend before my eyes. All was silent now. The massacre had ended. One hundred and seventy-six of the bravest men that the world ever saw had fallen and not one had asked for mercy. I walked out of the cell and when I stepped upon the floor of the Alamo the blood ran into my shoes."

*Enrique Esparza.* CN07557,
*De Zavala (Adina) Papers,*
*box 3Y28,*
*Center for American History,*
*University of Texas, Austin.*

- 23 -
Enrique Esparza
*San Antonio Light*
10 NOVEMBER 1901

*Young Enrique Esparza, whose father, Gregorio, died as an Alamo defender, accompanied his family within the walls of the Alamo during the siege and final assault. He was not widely recognized as an Alamo survivor until this published interview by local historian Adina de Zavala. De Zavala was the granddaughter of the first vice president of the Texas Republic and founded the De Zavala Society, a historical group that initiated the effort to preserve the Alamo and subsequently affiliated with the Daughters of the Republic of Texas. These childhood memories of the elderly Esparza recount the battle and the experience of the survivors afterward.*

### ANOTHER CHILD OF THE ALAMO
*Miss De Zavala Discovers a Man Who Was in the Fort When It Fell— His Father among the Massacred*

History says that only a woman and one child escaped from the massacre of the Alamo, but a San Antonio lady has made the discovery that history is wrong and that two children, whose parents were Texas soldiers, escaped besides a number of others who were non-participants.

The lady in question is Miss Adina De Zavala, [grand]daughter of the first vice president of the Republic of Texas. The child of the Alamo number two is now an old man, bowed with the weight of years, but his intellect is still as good as ever and Miss De Zavala expects to glean some very valuable data from him. He is a resident of this city and says he was only eight years of age at the time of the famous massacre, but he remembers vividly the scenes of carnage and bloodshed and relates them in a plain matter of fact way, without embellishment or an attempt at personal aggrandizement.

He is a Mexican and has kept silent all these years because he did not know the value of his testimony or think anything about the famous battle through which he went when he received his baptism of blood and fire. It was only accidentally that he was discovered by Miss De Zavala and she considers her find a remarkable one.

She says he told her things about the siege and fall of the famous "Cradle of Texas Liberty" that convince her beyond a doubt that he is no impostor. He has also given her data on things that occurred inside the famous old fort which history has always been at a loss to accurately chronicle and related other things which were not known to have occurred, but which are considered to have been feasible, and she has written a few of them for the *Light*, enough to show that her protege is not faking or shamming.

Miss De Zavala's article was handed the *Light* yesterday and besides the statement that this man was in the Alamo, her article says that there were a number of others who also were there and not massacred. They were Mexican refugees, however, and Miss De Zavala's recent find and the original "Child of the Alamo" [Angelina Dickinson] are the only known ones to escape, whose fathers were of the doomed Texas garrison.

This man whom Miss De Zavala has discovered is Don Enrique Esparza and his photograph, which she also handed the *Light*, shows him to be a man of apparently more than ordinary intellect, a strong, robust, honest looking old fellow. His father, he says, was a Texas soldier who fell in the defense of the sacred fort. Notwithstanding this, he says his father's body was not burned with the other slaughtered Texas patriots, but that a friend [relative] in the Mexican army secured it and that it was interred. He gives the names of the others who were in the Alamo and among them are some families yet known in this vicinity. The Alsbury family is mentioned for one. Grandchildren of this family reside in or near San Antonio. Tom is a farmer east of the city and Perry lives here, having until recently been on the city carpenters' force. It has always been known that an Alsbury was in the garrison and this man's familiarity with this and other subjects known already, convinces Miss De Zavala that he is not an impostor and that he knows whereof he speaks.

Esparza tells Miss De Zavala that he and the other Mexicans who escaped from the butchery of Santa Anna's hordes were concealed in two store rooms in the courtyard of the Alamo proper, in front of what is left of the old building, and that these rooms were on each side of the main entrance gate which led into the court from the outside. He also says the walls were surrounded on the outside by a ditch "as deep as two men" and that a drawbridge spanning this moat afforded the means of ingress and egress to and from the place. It is known that such a wall and moat did exist and Esparza's apparent familiarity with this is another proof of the genuineness of his story.

Another thing. Miss De Zavala and numerous other students of Texas history have contended all along that Madam Candelaria [Andrea Castañón Villanueva], the old Mexican woman who recently died, claiming to have been in the Alamo when it fell, was not really there. Miss De Zavala even says Madam Candelaria did not herself claim to have been in the Alamo at its fall until a few years before her death. Esparza says she was not there. She had been in it frequently before it fell, he says, and was there immediately afterward, but was not present when the actual fall of the Alamo and massacre of its patriotic defenders occurred.

Miss De Zavala's statement regarding her find, as handed the *Light*, is as follows:

Don Enrique Esparza, who is still living, was an eyewitness to some of the most tragic scenes of the past century. He was a child of eight at the time of the massacre of the Alamo. His eyes are bright and his memory clear. He had the advantage of a good education and is most entertaining.

His father, too, lived in terrible days—was captured as a child by the Comanche Indians and was ransomed after he was grown by Colonel [José Francisco?] Ruiz and brought back to San Antonio. The families of both parents of Esparza were well-to-do and intelligent people and chose to fight for freedom and the Constitution of 1824.

Early in 1836 they were warned by letters from Vice President [Lorenzo] de Zavala, through Captain [Francisco?] Rojo, that the Mexican hordes were coming and advised to take their families to a place of safety. No wagons were obtainable and so they waited. On the morning of February 22, John W. Smith, one of the scouts, galloped up to Esparza's house bearing the news that Santa Anna was near—would be upon them by night. What should they do? was the question. Fly they could not! Should they try and hide or go into the fortress of the Alamo? The Alamo was decided upon by the mother as there her husband would be fighting for liberty. There they carried in their arms their most precious possessions—going back and forth many times, till at sunset the mother, Mrs. Anita Esparza, with her last bundles and her little daughter and four sons, passed across the bridge over the *acequia* [canal] into the courtyard of the Alamo just as the trumpet's blare and noise of Santa Anna's army was heard. Within the Alamo courtyard were also other refugees who were saved—Mrs. [Juana Navarro] Alsbury and one child and sister, Gertrudes Navarro; Mrs. Concepción Losoya, her daughter and two sons; Victoriana de Salina and three little girls; Mrs. [Susanna] Dickinson and baby (hitherto believed to have been the only ones who escaped alive); and an old woman called Petra.

No tongue can describe the terror and horror of that fearful last fight! The women and children were paralyzed with terror and faint from hunger when the Mexican soldiers rushed in after the fall of the Alamo. A poor paralytic unable to speak to them and tell that he was not a belligerent was murdered before their eyes, as was also a young fellow who had been captured sometime previous and continued in the Alamo. Brigidio Guerrero, a youth, was saved as he managed to say he was not a Texan, but a Texan prisoner.

A Mexican officer, related to some of the refugees, arrived just in time to save the women and children—but they were subjected to terrible usage and horrible abuse. Finally, someone obtained safe conduct for them at about two o'clock on the morning of the 7th to the house of Governor [Ramón] Músquiz, on Main Plaza. Here the famished prisoners were served with coffee by the Músquiz domestics. At daylight they were required to go before Santa Anna and take the oath of allegiance. Each mother was then given a blanket and two dollars by Santa Anna in person. The only two who escaped this additional humiliation were the two daughters of Navarro, who were spirited away from Músquiz's house by their father [uncle]—José Antonio Navarro. The body of Esparza's father, who was butchered with other Texans, was obtained by his brother who was in the Mexican army and was buried in the San Fernando Campo Santo [cemetery] and thus he has the distinction of being the only Texan who escaped the funeral pyre.

Miss De Zavala thinks that from what she can glean from Esparza, she can add much valuable information to history about the fall of the Alamo, of which very little is now authentically known. No Texas history mentions the escape of anyone from the Alamo but Mrs. Dickinson and child, and the San Antonio lady's discovery is of great value.

- 24 -

Enrique Esparza

*San Antonio Express*

22 NOVEMBER 1902

*Newspaper reporters published several interviews of Enrique Esparza during the early twentieth century. Like an earlier Esparza account (see document 23), these childhood memories of the elderly Esparza recount the battle and the experience of the survivors afterward. They also narrate additional events that*

*occurred during the siege. This text is the interviewer's translation of Esparza's
Spanish commentary.*

## THE STORY OF ENRIQUE ESPARZA
*Says That He Was in the Siege of the Alamo*
Is Seventy-four Years Old and Tells an Interesting Tale
of That Memorable Massacre and Scenes Leading Up to It

Since the death of Señora [Andrea Castañón] Candelaria Villanueva several years ago at the age of 113 [95] there is but one person alive who claims
to have been in the siege of the Alamo. That person is Enrique Esparza,
now seventy-four years old, who, firm-stepped, clear-minded and clear-eyed,
bids fair to live to the age of the woman who for so long shared honors
with him.

Enrique Esparza, who tells one of the most interesting stories ever narrated, works a truck garden on Nogalitos Street between the Southern Pa-
cific Railroad track and the San Pedro Creek. Here he lives with the family
of his son, Victor Esparza. Every morning he is up before daybreak and
helps load the wagons with garden stuff that is to be taken uptown to
market.

He is a farmer of experience and contributes very materially to the suc-
cess of the beautiful five acre garden, of which he is the joint proprietor.

While claims of Enrique Esparza have been known among those familiar with the historical work done by the Daughters of the Republic, an
organization which has taken great interest in getting first-hand information of the period of Texas independence, the old man was not available up
to about five years ago, for the reason that he resided on his farm in Atascosa
County. This accounts for the fact that he is not well enough known to be
included in the itinerary when San Antonians are proudly doing the town
with their friends.

Esparza tells a straight story. Although he is a Mexican, his gentleness
and unassuming frankness are like the typical old Texan. Every syllable he
speaks is uttered with confidence and in his tale he frequently makes di-
gressions, going into details of relationship of early families of San Antonio
and showing a tenacious memory. At the time of the fight of the Alamo he
was eight years old. His father was a defender and his father's own brother
an assailant of the Alamo. He was a witness of his mother's grief and had

his own grief at the slaughter in which his father was included. As he narrated to a reporter the events in which he was so deeply concerned his voice several times choked and he could not proceed for emotion. While he has a fair idea of English, he preferred to talk in Spanish.

### Esparza's Story.

My father, Gregorio Esparza, belonged to [Placido] Benavides' company in the American army and I think it was in February 1836 that the company was ordered to Corpus Christi. They had gotten to Goliad when my father was ordered back alone to San Antonio, for what I don't know. When he got here there were rumors that Santa Anna was on the way here and many residents sent their families away. One of my father's friends told him that he could have a wagon and team and all necessary provisions for a trip if he wanted to take his family away. There were six of us besides my father: my mother, whose name was Anita, my elder sister, myself and three younger brothers, one a baby in arms. I was eight years old.

My father decided to take the offer and move the family to San Felipe. Everything was ready when one morning Mr. [John] W. Smith, who was godfather to my youngest brother, came to our house on North Flores Street just above where the Presbyterian Church now is and told my mother to tell my father when he came in that Santa Anna had come.

When my father came my mother asked him what he would do. You know the Americans had the Alamo, which had been fortified a few months before by General [Martín] Cos.

"Well, I'm going to the fort," my father said.

"Well, if you go, I'm going along, and the whole family too."

It took the whole day to move and an hour before sundown we were inside the fort. There was a bridge over the river about where Commerce Street crosses it and just as we got to it we could hear Santa Anna's drums beating on Milam Square; and just as we were crossing the ditch going into the fort Santa Anna fired his salute on Milam Square.

There were a few other families who had gone in. A Mrs. [Juana Navarro] Alsbury and her sister; a Mrs. Victoriana and a family of several girls, two of whom I knew afterwards; Mrs. [Susanna] Dickinson; Mrs. Juana Melton, a Mexican woman who had married an American; also a woman named Concepción Losoya and her son, Juan, who was a little older than I.

The first thing I remember after getting inside the fort was seeing Mrs. Melton making circles on the ground with an umbrella. I had seen very few umbrellas. While I was walking around about dark I went near a man named [Antonio] Fuentes who was talking at a distance with a soldier. When the latter got near me he said to Fuentes: "Did you know they had cut the water off?"

The fort was built around a square. The present Hugo-Schmeltzer building is part of it. I remember the main entrance was on the south side of the large enclosure. The quarters were not in the church, but on the south side of the fort on either side of the entrance, and were part of the convent. There was a ditch of running water back of the church and another along the west side of Alamo Plaza. We couldn't get to the latter ditch as it was under fire and it was the other one that Santa Anna cut off. The next morning after we had gotten in the fort I saw the men drawing water from a well that was in the convent yard. The well was located a little south of the center of the square. I don't know whether it is there now or not.

On the first night a company of which my father was one went out and captured some prisoners. One of them was a Mexican soldier and all through the siege he interpreted the bugle calls on the Mexican side and in this way the Americans kept posted on the movements of the enemy.

After the first day there was fighting every day. The Mexicans had a cannon somewhere near where Dwyer Avenue now is and every fifteen minutes they dropped a shot into the fort.

The roof of the Alamo had been taken off and the south side filled up with dirt almost to the roof on that side so that there was a slanting embankment up which the Americans could run and take positions. During the fight I saw numbers who were shot in the head as soon as they exposed themselves from the roof. There were holes made in the walls of the fort and the Americans continually shot from these also. We also had two cannon, one at the main entrance and one at the northwest corner of the fort near the post office. The cannon were seldom fired.

*Remembers Crockett.*

I remember Crockett. He was a tall, slim man with black whiskers. He was always at the head. The Mexicans called him Don Benito. The Americans said he was Crockett. He would often come to the fire and warm his hands and say a few words to us in the Mexican language. I also remember hearing the names of Travis and Bowie mentioned, but I never saw either of them that I know of.

After the first few days I remember that a messenger came from somewhere with word that help was coming. The Americans celebrated it by beating the drums and playing on the flute. But after about seven days fighting there was an armistice of three days and during this time Don Benito had conferences every day with Santa Anna. Badio [Juan A. Badillo], the interpreter, was a close friend of my father and I heard him tell my father in the quarters that Santa Anna had offered to let the Americans go with their lives if they would surrender, but the Mexicans would be treated as rebels.

During the armistice my father told my mother she had better take the children and go, while she could do so safely. But my mother said: "No! If you're going to stay, so am I. If they kill one they can kill us all."

Only one person went out during the armistice, a woman named Trinidad Saucedo.

Don Benito, or Crockett, as the Americans called him, assembled the men on the last day and told them Santa Anna's terms, but none of them believed that anyone who surrendered would get out alive, so they all said as they would have to die anyhow they would fight it out.

The fighting began again and continued every day and nearly every night. One night there was music in the Mexican camp and the Mexican prisoner said it meant that reinforcements had arrived.

We then had another messenger who got through the lines, saying that communication had been cut off and the promised reinforcements could not be sent.

### The Last Night.

On the last night my father was not out, but he and my mother were sleeping together in headquarters. About two o'clock in the morning there was a great shooting and firing at the northwest corner of the fort and I heard my mother say: "Gregorio, the soldiers have jumped the wall. The fight's begun."

He got up and picked up his arms and went into the fight. I never saw him again. My uncle told me afterwards that Santa Anna gave him permission to get my father's body and that he found it where the thick of the fight had been.

We could hear the Mexican officers shouting to the men to jump over and the men were fighting so close that we could hear them strike each other. It was so dark that we couldn't see anything and the families that were in the quarters just huddled up in the corners. My mother's children were near her. Finally they began shooting through the dark into the room where we were. A boy who was wrapped in a blanket in one corner was hit and killed. The Mexicans fired into the room for at least fifteen minutes. It was a miracle, but none of us children were touched.

By daybreak the firing had almost stopped and through the window we could see shadows of men moving around inside the fort. The Mexicans went from room to room looking for an American to kill. While it was still dark a man stepped into the room and pointed his bayonet at my mother's breast, demanding: "Where's the money the Americans had?"

"If they had any," said my mother, "you may look for it."

Then an officer stepped in and said: "What are you doing? The women and children are not to be hurt."

The officer then told my mother to pick out her own family and get her belongings, and the other women were given the same instructions. When it was broad day the Mexicans began to remove the dead. There were so many killed that it took several days to carry them away.

The families with their baggage were then sent under guard to the house of Don Ramón Músquiz, which was located where Frank Brothers Store now is, on Main Plaza. Here we were given coffee and some food and were told that we would go before the president at two o'clock. On our way to the Músquiz house we passed up Commerce Street and it was crowded as far as Presa Street with soldiers who did not fire a shot during the battle. Santa Anna had many times more troops than he could use.

At three o'clock we went before Santa Anna. His quarters were in a house which stood where [Saul] Wolfson's store now is. He had a great stack of silver money on a table before him and a pile of blankets. One by one the women were sent into a side room to make their declaration and on coming out were given two dollars and a blanket. While my mother was waiting her turn Mrs. Melton, who had never recognized my mother as an acquaintance and who was considered an aristocrat, sent her brother, Juan Losoya, across the room to my mother to ask the favor that nothing be said to the president about her marriage with an American.

My mother told Juan to tell her not to be afraid.

Mrs. Dickinson was there, also several other women. After the president had given my mother her two dollars and blanket, he told her she was free to go where she liked. We gathered what belongings we could together and went to our cousin's place on North Flores Street, where we remained several months.

*Pablo Díaz.* CN08092, San Antonio Light, *31 October 1909, 10, Texas Newspaper Collection, Center for American History, University of Texas, Austin.*

- 25 -

Pablo Díaz
*San Antonio Express*
1 JULY 1906

*Pablo Díaz was a young man at the time of the Alamo battle. He was not in the town of San Antonio during the hostilities but heard the booming cannons and rattle of musketry in the distance. He also witnessed local events before and after the battle. In this account recorded by newspaper reporter Charles Merritt Barnes, the elderly Díaz recalled the Texan fortifications of the Alamo, the funeral pyres of the Alamo defenders, and the gruesome spectacle of Mexican corpses floating in the river. Barnes began working as an* Express *reporter around 1880. During the first decade of the twentieth century, he wrote numerous feature articles on topics of local interest.*

## AGED CITIZEN DESCRIBES ALAMO FIGHT AND FIRE
*Pablo Díaz, Now Ninety Years of Age, Relates Story of Alamo as He Saw It Next Day*
How the River Was Filled with Bodies

To have seen the ashes of those who were slain in the Alamo is an experience that but few men now living can claim. There is one man living in San Antonio who makes this claim. He does so with all the appearances and indications of his contention being correct. He seems not only to know the place where the heroes' corpses were burned, but gives a vivid description of the occurrence and his experience and positively points out and locates the spot, as well as the one where the few charred bones that were left were interred.

This man is Pablo Díaz. He lives with his niece, Alcaria Cypriana, on the west side of the Alazán Creek near the old San Fernando Cemetery. He is nearly ninety years old. He tells a very interesting story. He says:

I was born in Monclova, Mexico. Myself and my brother, Francisco Díaz, who is my senior by about eight years, had heard a great deal about the beauty of San Antonio. We were both very young then, he in his twenties and I still in my teens. We had both learned the trade of carpenter, and as wages in Monclova were very small we concluded to come here.

After many narrow escapes we finally reached here in February 1835. Not very long after our arrival [Stephen F.] Austin and [Edward] Burleson with their forces came to the vicinity of San Antonio and located their camp near the head of the San Antonio River, and later at the Molino Blanco. Along about that time Captain Juan N. Seguín was recruiting a company to join Austin's force of Constitutionalists, as the American colonists were called. Seguín prevailed on my brother, Francisco, to enlist in his company and the latter endeavored to induce me to join them, but I did not. I held that, having been born in Mexico, it was not right for me to take up arms against my native land, but I held that as I was living in this country it was not right for me to fight against it, so I became strictly neutral and took no part on either side.

I have since regretted, however, that I did not join the Constitutionalists or Texans, for when I saw and realized the cruelties and enormities perpetrated by the invading armies from Mexico and the brutal treatment they accorded to the innocent women and children I could not help feeling ashamed and held aloof. I had not been here very long before General [Martín] Cos and his army from Mexico came here. I was too young to have been impressed or conscripted into its service . . .

After Cos surrendered [in December 1835] that portion of the army of the Constitutionalists that remained for a while was quartered in the barracks vacated by the Mexicans on Military Plaza, but soon after the arrival of Davy Crockett the small band moved over to the Alamo because the defenses were better and more substantial than the ones on the west side of the city. The weakness of the military fortress or *presidio*, as it was called, on Military Plaza had been demonstrated by the facility with which [Ben] Milam's forces had dislodged the soldiers under General Cos. As soon as the coming of Santa Anna, which had been heralded, was known the Constitutionalists retired to the Alamo and commenced to fortify it. Up to this time it had not been used as a military fortification, but was a church and convent.

The arrival of Santa Anna was announced by the firing of a gun from in front of the *alcalde's* [mayor's] house on Main Plaza. His red flag was hoisted over the cathedral. I heard the gun fired from the plaza and saw the flag floating from San Fernando. From the mission [Concepción] I could see also the flag of the Constitutionalists floating from the Alamo. The latter flag was not the flag that was afterward adopted by the Texas Republic, with its blue field and single star and a stripe of white and one of red, but was the flag of Mexico under the Constitution and prior to the usurpation and assumption of the dictatorship by Santa Anna. When Santa Anna hoisted his red flag it was his announcement that no quarter would be shown those opposing him. This was well understood by those in the Alamo. They knew that unless Houston, on whom they vainly relied, sent them succor they were lost.

### Díaz Saw the Terrible Carnage.

For six days I heard the rattle of musketry and the roar of cannon. I did not dare to leave my refuge near the mission lest I become involved in the terrible slaughter which I knew was going on there. Messengers frequently came out to the mission and told us of the terrible devastation and butchery in progress and of the brave and dauntless defense of the heroic Constitutionalists. The cannon shots became louder and more frequent as Santa Anna's soldiers got closer and closer to the Alamo. Finally, on the sixth day, after a fierce fusillade, there was silence and I saw the red flag of Santa Anna floating from the Alamo where the Constitutional flag before had been. Then I knew that the battle was over, that the invading tyrant and his horde had won and that the price paid for their stubborn defense by the Constitutionalists had been their lives. I had several personal friends among the brave men in the Alamo. One of them was named [Agapito] Cervantes. His descendants lived on the Alameda for many years and some of them are now residing on Losoya Street.

Next I saw an immense pillar of flame shoot up a short distance to the south and east of the Alamo and the dense smoke from it rose high into the clouds. I saw it burn for two days and nights and then flame and smoke subsided and smoldered. I left my retreat and came forth cautiously, coming along Garden Street to town. I noticed that the air was tainted with the terrible odor from many corpses and I saw thousands of vultures flying above me. As I reached the ford of the river my gaze encountered a terrible sight. The stream was congested with the corpses that had been thrown into it. The *alcalde*, [Francisco Antonio] Ruiz, had vainly endeavored to bury the bodies of the soldiers of Santa Anna who had been slain by the defenders of the Alamo. He had exhausted all of his resources and still was unable to cope with the task. There were too many of them. Nearly six thousand of Santa Anna's ten thousand had fallen before they annihilated their adversaries and captured their fortress. I halted, horrified, and watched the vultures in their revel and shuddered at the sickening sight. Then involuntarily I put my hands before my eyes and turned away from the river, which I hesitated to cross. Hurriedly I turned aside and up La Villita and went to South Alamo. I could not help seeing the corpses which congested the river all around the bend from Garden to way above Commerce Street and as far as Crockett Street is now.

They stayed there for many days until finally the *alcalde* got a force sufficient to dislodge them and float them down the river. But while this was a most gruesome sight, the one I saw later filled me with more horror. I went on to the Alameda. It was then a broad and spacious, irregularly shaped place, flanked on both sides with huge cottonwood trees, from which it gets its name. I turned into the Alameda at the present intersection of Commerce and Alamo Streets. Looking eastward I saw a large crowd gathered. Intuitively I went to the place.

*He Saw the Ashes of the Heroes.*
It was just beyond where the Ludlow now stands. The crowd was gathered around the smoldering embers and ashes of the fire that I had seen from the mission. It was here that the *alcalde* had ordered the bodies of Bowie, of Crockett, Travis and all of their dauntless comrades who had been slain in the Alamo's unequal combat to be brought and burned. I did not need to make inquiry. The story was told by the silent witnesses before me. Fragments of flesh, bones and charred wood and ashes revealed it in all of its terrible truth. Grease that had exuded from the bodies saturated the earth for several feet beyond the ashes and smoldering mesquite fagots. The odor was more sickening than that from the corpses in the river. I turned my head aside and left the place in shame.

At this juncture of his story the venerable patriarch Díaz stopped and pointed out the spot to me. I had got Ben Fisk to interpret the first part of it for me, after which I had asked Díaz to go with me and show me the spot that I might know its exact location. Antonio Pérez accompanied us, Fisk being unable to go with us. We left the car at the point indicated by Díaz. He first took us to the old Post House, where it had been stated to me by another person that the bodies had been buried. To this Díaz replied: "The pyre was a very long one, as it had to consume nearly two hundred corpses, and it may be that some of the bodies may not have been burned in the main one, but have been burned on the opposite of the Alameda, but if they were I did not see the ashes. I am not prepared to say there were no bodies burned anywhere but at the spot I shall indicate and it is not unlikely that they were burned here. It is probable that all of the bodies were not carried away from the Alamo at the same time or the Constitutionalists all separated from the Federals at the same time, so the story that some of the bodies were burned on the south side of the Alameda and where stands the Post House belonging to Dr. [Ferdinand] Herff Sr. and now called the Springfield House may be true. But the main funeral pyre was about two hundred yards east of where St. Joseph's Church now stands and just beyond this big red brick house (meaning the Ludlow) and thence for fifty to sixty yards north."

The spot was then pointed out to me by Señor Díaz and I have it now definitely located in my mind. The location is confirmed by Pérez, who states that when he was a little boy and used to play on the Alameda he was frequently shown the same spot as the place where the bodies of the Alamo heroes were burned. Pérez goes further than Díaz and says that for many years there was a small mound there under which he was told the charred bones that the fire did not consume were buried by some humane persons, who had to do so secretly, and that he was familiar with the spot as the burial place of Bowie and Crockett. Pérez states that about thirty years ago these bones were exhumed and placed in the old City Cemetery, the first one located on the Powder House Hill, but he does not know the part of that cemetery they were placed in. Díaz when told that no monument had ever been erected to the memory of any of the heroes, except the one started, but never completed, that stands above the spot where Milam is finally buried, said: "It is a great shame to be forced to admit that neither the state nor the United States have ever erected a monument. It is to be hoped that a suitable and imposing one may be placed on the Alameda to mark the place where the bodies of those heroes were burned and I hope you will remember the spot and endeavor to get someone to so mark it."

*Charles Merritt Barnes*

- 26 -

Enrique Esparza
*San Antonio Express*
12, 19 MAY 1907

*Enrique Esparza's 1907 account is much longer and more detailed than his earlier reminiscences (see documents 23 and 24). Recorded by Charles Merritt Barnes (see document 25), these recollections from Esparza's childhood memories encompass the siege, battle, final assault, and aftermath of the Alamo, as well as the subsequent history of the site and some personal observations on Travis, Bowie, and Crockett.*

# ALAMO'S ONLY SURVIVOR

*Enrique Esparza, Who Claims to Have Been There During the Siege, Tells the Story of the Fall*

At 707 Nogalitos Street there stands a small cottage, covered with madeira and trumpet vines which cling to its eaves and cluster along its porch. Roses and myrtle grow beside and in front. Nearby figs and other fruits grow, while all about is green and shady or tinted with the blooms of fragrant and many colored flowers that grow there in profusion.

This humble cottage shelters the only living being now claiming to have been within the walls of the Alamo when it was besieged by Santa Anna's horde and fell under their deadly fire. Although confessing that eighty-two [seventy-eight?] years have passed since he was born, he is yet hale and strong. He owns the small *suerte* [plot] of land on which his lowly home stands and when I saw him this week with a team he was tilling its soil. His name is Enrique Esparza. The story he tells is marvelous. He speaks English admirably and nothing he says is marred but is emphasized by his mode of speech. This is his story:

All of the others are dead. I alone live of they who were within the Alamo when it fell. There is none other left now to tell its story and when I go to sleep my last slumber in the *campo de los santos* [cemetery] there will then be no one left to tell.

You ask me do I remember it. I tell you yes. It is burned into my brain and indelibly seared there. Neither age nor infirmity could make me forget, for the scene was one of such horror that it could never be forgotten by anyone who witnessed its incidents.

I was born in one of the old adobe houses that formerly stood on the east side of what we then called El Calle de [la] Acequia or the street of the *acequia* or ditch, but now known as Main Avenue. The house in which I was born was but a short distance north of Salinas Street. I am the son of Gregorio Esparza.

You will see my father's name on the list of those who died in the Alamo. This list is at Austin. It is on the monument in front of the Capitol. That monument was built there in honor of those who fell with the Alamo. I have made several pilgrimages to it just to read the inscription and list of names because my father's name is on the list. There is no monument here to those who fell in the Alamo and died there that Texas might be free. There are none here with the means to do so who have ever cared enough for those who died there to mark the spot where their bodies were buried. Though this be so, those who died there were all brave, both men and women.

My mother was also in the Alamo when it fell, as were some of my brothers and a sister. My mother's maiden name was Anna Salazar. She told me I was born in the month of September and in the year 1824 [1828?].

*Went into the Alamo.*

I was then a boy of twelve [eight?] years of age; was then quite small and delicate and could have passed for a child of eight. My father was a friend and comrade of [John] William Smith. Smith had expected to send my father and our family away with his own family in a wagon to Nacogdoches. We were waiting for the wagon to be brought to town. My father and Smith had heard of the approach of Santa Anna, but did not expect him and his forces to arrive as early as they did. Santa Anna and his men got here before the wagon we waited for could come.

My father was told by Smith that all who were friends to the Americans had better join the Americans who had taken refuge in the Alamo. Smith and his family went there and my father and his family went with them.

Santa Anna and his army arrived at about sundown and almost immediately after we sought refuge in the Alamo. Immediately after their arrival Santa Anna's personal staff dismounted on Main Plaza in front of the San Fernando Church. Santa Anna went into the building at the northwest corner of Main Plaza which has since been superseded by that now occupied by S[aul] Wolfson. That building had been occupied by the Texans and before them by the soldiers of Mexico and still earlier by the soldiers of Spain. It had been a part of the *presidio*, or old fort, and the part where the officers had their headquarters. The Texans had left this structure and gone over to the Alamo because the latter offered more advantages for defense.

I have often heard it said that Santa Anna immediately upon his arrival in San Antonio dismounted in the west side of Military Plaza and hitched his horse to an iron ring set into the wall of the old building where the Spanish governors dwelt and where the combined coats of arms of Spain and Austria form the keystone of the arch above its portal. This is not so. I saw Santa Anna when he arrived. I saw him dismount. He did not hitch the horse. He gave its bridle reins to a lackey. He and his staff proceeded immediately to the house on the northwest corner of Main Plaza. I was playing with some other children on the plaza and when Santa Anna and his soldiers came up we ran off and told our parents, who almost immediately afterward took me and the other children of the family to the Alamo. I am sure of this for I saw Santa Anna several times afterward and after I came out of the Alamo.

### Within the Walls of the Alamo.

It was twilight when we got into the Alamo and it grew pitch dark soon afterward. All of the doors were closed and barred. The sentinels that had been on duty without were first called inside and then the openings closed. Some sentinels were posted upon the roof, but these were protected by the walls of the Alamo church and the old convent building. We went into the church portion. It was shut up when we arrived. We were admitted through a small window.

I distinctly remember that I climbed through the window and over a cannon that was placed inside of the church immediately behind the window. There were several other cannon there. Some were back of the doors. Some had been mounted on the roof and some had been placed in the convent. The window was opened to permit us to enter and it was closed immediately after we got inside.

We had not been in there long when a messenger came from Santa Anna calling on us to surrender. I remember the reply to this summons was a shot from one of the cannon on the roof of the Alamo. Soon after it was fired I heard Santa Anna's cannon reply. I heard his cannon shot strike the walls of the church and also the convent. Then I heard the cannon within the Alamo buildings, both church and convent, fire repeatedly during the night. I heard the cheers of the Alamo gunners and the deriding jeers of Santa Anna's troops.

My heart quaked when the shot tore through the timbers. My fear and terror were overwhelming, but my brave mother and my dauntless father sought to soothe and quiet my brothers and myself. My sister was but an infant and knew naught of the tragic scenes enacted about us. But even child as I was I could not help but feel inspired by the bravery of the heroes about me.

*Would Have Fought Also.*

If I had been given a weapon I would have fought likewise. But weapons and ammunition were scarce and only wielded and used by those who knew how. But I saw some there no older than I who had them and fought as bravely and died as stolidly as the adults. This was towards the end and when many of the grown persons within had been slain by the foes without. It was then that some of the children joined in the defense.

All who had weapons used them as often as they had the chance to do so; shots were fired fast. Bullets flew thick. Both men and women fell within the walls. Even children died there. The fighting was intermittent. We must have been within the Alamo ten or twelve days. I did not count the days. But they were long and full of terror. The nights were longer and fraught with still more horror. It was between the periods of fierce fighting and all too short armistice that we got any rest.

Crockett seemed to be the leading spirit. He was everywhere. He went to every exposed point and personally directed the fighting. Travis was chief in command, but he depended more upon the judgment of Crockett and that brave man's intrepidity than upon his own. Bowie, too, was brave and dauntless, but he was ill. Prone upon his cot he was unable to see much that was going on about him and the others were too engrossed to stop and tell him. Although too weak to stand upon his feet, when Travis drew the line with his sword Bowie [had] those around him bring his cot across the line.

I heard the few Mexicans there call Crockett "Don Benito." Afterward I learned his name was David, but I only knew him as "Don Benito."

*Those Who Left.*

One day when I went to where Bowie was lying on his cot I heard him call those about him and say: "All of you who desire to leave here may go in safety. Santa Anna has just sent a message to Travis saying there will be an armistice for three days to give us time to deliberate on surrendering. During these three days all who desire to do so may go out of here. Travis has sent me the message and told me to tell those near me."

When Bowie said this quite a number left. Travis and Bowie took advantage of this occasion to send out for succor they vainly hoped would come to the Alamo and those within before it fell. [John] William Smith and [Horatio Alexander] Alsbury were among those who were sent for succor then. Seguín claimed also to have been so sent. Among the surnames of those I remember to have left during the time of this armistice were [Antonio] Menchaca, [Manuel?] Flores, [Ambrosio?] Rodríguez, [Eduardo?] Ramírez, [Antonio Cruz] Arocha, [?] Silvero. They are now all dead. Among the women who went out were some of their relatives.

[Louis] Rose left after this armistice had expired and after the others had been sent for succor. Rose went out after Travis drew the line with his sword. He was the only man who did not cross the line. Up to then he had fought as bravely as any man there. He had stood by the cannon.

Rose went out during the night. They opened a window for him and let him go. The others who left before went out of the doors and in the daytime. Alsbury left his wife and sister-in-law there. His sister-in-law afterward married a man named [Juan N.] Cantú. She and Mrs. [Juana Navarro] Alsbury stayed in the Alamo until it fell. They feared to leave, believing the Mexicans under Santa Anna would kill them.

Bowie asked my father if he wished to go when the armistice of three days was on. My father replied: "No. I will stay and die fighting."

My mother then said: "I will stay by your side and with our children die too. They will soon kill us. We will not linger in pain."

So we stayed. And so my father died, as he said, fighting. He struck down one of his foes as he fell in the heap of slain.

### How the End Came.

The end came suddenly and almost unexpectedly and with a rush. It came at night and when all was dark save when there was a gleam of light from the flash and flame of a fired gun. Our men fought hard all day long. Their ammunition was very low. That of many was entirely spent. Santa Anna must have known this, for his men had been able during the day to make several breeches in the walls. Our men had fought long and hard and well. But their strength was spent. Many slept. Few there were who were awake. Even those on guard besides the breeches in the walls dozed. The fire from the Mexicans had slacked and finally ceased. Those who were awake saw the Mexican foemen lying quietly by their campfires and thought they likewise slept. But our foes were only simulating sleep or, if they slept, were awakened by their savage chief and his brutal officers.

After all had been dark and quiet for many hours and I had fallen into a profound slumber suddenly there was a terrible din. Cannon boomed. Their shot crashed through the doors and windows and the breeches in the walls. Then men rushed in on us. They swarmed among us and over us. They fired on us in volleys. They struck us down with their *escopetas* [muskets]. In the dark our men groped and grasped the throats of our foemen and buried their knives into their hearts.

*A Boy Hero.*

By my side was an American boy. He was about my own age but larger. As they reached us he rose to his feet. He had been sleeping but, like myself, he had been rudely awakened. As they rushed upon him he stood calmly and across his shoulders drew the blanket on which he had slept. He was unarmed. They slew him where he stood and his corpse fell over me. My father's body was lying near the cannon which he had tended. My mother with my baby sister was kneeling beside it. My brothers and I were close to her. I clutched her garments. Behind her crouched the only man who escaped and was permitted to surrender. His name was Brigidio Guerrero.

As they rushed upon us the Mexican soldiers faltered as they saw a woman. My mother clasped her babe to her breast and closed her eyes. She expected they would kill her and her babe and me and my brothers. I thought so too. My blood ran cold and I grew faint and sick.

Brigidio Guerrero pled for mercy. He told them he was a prisoner in the Alamo and had been brought there against his will. He said he had tried to escape and join Santa Anna's men. They spared him. They led him out, an officer going with him.

They took my mother, her babe, my brothers and I to another part of the building where there were other women and children all huddled. Another of the women had a babe at her breast. This was Mrs. [Susanna] Dickinson. There was an old woman in there. They called her Doña Petra. This was the only name I ever knew her by. With her was a young girl, Trinidad Saucedo, who was very beautiful. Mrs. [Juana Navarro] Alsbury and her sister were there also and several other women, young girls and little boys. I do not remember having seen Madam Candelaria [Andrea Castañón Villanueva] there. She may have been among the women and I may not have noticed her particularly. She claimed to have been there and I shall not dispute her word. I did not notice the women as closely as I did the men.

*Fired After All Were Killed.*

After the soldiers of Santa Anna had got in a corner all of the women and children who had not been killed in the onslaught, they kept firing on the men who had defended the Alamo. For fully a quarter of an hour they kept firing upon them after all of the defenders had been slain and their corpses were lying still. It was pitch dark in the eastern end of the structure and the soldiers of Santa Anna seemed to fear to go there even after firing from the Constitutionalists from there had ceased. Santa Anna's men stood still and fired into the darkness and until someone brought lanterns.

The last I saw of my father's corpse was when one of them held his lantern above it and over the dead who lay about the cannon he had tended.

It has been stated that one of the women who claims to have been in the Alamo during its siege and capture has also claimed that she brought water into the Alamo from the ditch outside. This is not true. When we got into the Alamo, which was before access to the ditch had been entirely cut off by the soldiers of Santa Anna, such occurrence had been foreseen and forestalled by inmates of the Alamo chapel. They had already sunk a well in the church and the water therefrom was then being drunk by the occupants instead of the water from the ditch. A number of cattle had also been driven into the court of the convent. These latter furnished food for the besieged up to the day of the fall of the Alamo. I do not recollect the inmates having suffered for either food or water during the entire period of the siege. The only article that was scarce was ammunition. This got scarcer and scarcer each day, with no chance or hope of replenishing.

*Tells How Crockett Died.*

The old convent had been used for barracks by Bowie, Travis and Crockett's men and was so used until the besiegers had driven them to seek final refuge in the chapel after a number of breeches had been made in the convent wall. Communication was constantly kept up between the convent and the church buildings. This was done through a door connecting them. I was in the convent several times but stayed most, and practically all, of the time in the church, as it was considered safest. Crockett, who as I said before they called Don Benito, went often into the convent and stayed there for some time. But he was everywhere during the siege and personally slew many of the enemy with his rifle, his pistol and his knife. He fought hand to hand. He clubbed his rifle when they closed in on him and knocked them down with its stock until he was overwhelmed by numbers and slain. He fought to his last breath. He fell immediately in front of the large double doors which he defended with the force that was by his side. Crockett was one of the few who were wide awake when the final crisis and crash came. When he died there was a heap of slain in front [of] and on each side of him. These he had all killed before he finally fell on top of the heap.

Travis spent most of his time directing the firing from the roof of the church. He, too, seemed not only dauntless but sleepless. He encouraged the gunners. Whenever a good shot was made with the cannon he commended them. He told them where to aim and when to fire efficaciously, the cannon fire from the roof of the church being most of the time under his direct personal supervision. Crockett and he both, however, looked after the cannonading from the convent as well, both making repeated visits to that locality and at frequent intervals.

Bowie, although ill and suffering from a fever, fought until he was so severely wounded that he had to be carried to his cot, which was placed in one of the smaller rooms on the north side of the church. Even after he was confined to his cot he fought, firing his pistol and occasionally his rifle at the enemy after the soldiers of Santa Anna had entered the church and some of them got into his room. He loaded and fired his weapons until his foes closed in on him. When they made their final rush upon him, he rose up in his bed and received them. He buried his sharp bowie knife into the breast of one of them as another fired the shot that killed him. He was literally riddled with bullets. I saw his corpse before we were taken out of the building.

*Women Who Nursed Bowie.*
Mrs. [Juana Navarro] Alsbury and my mother were among those who nursed and ministered to his wants. Mrs. Alsbury was near him when he was killed, while my mother and I were in the large main room of the church and by the cannon near the window, where my father fell.

The shot and shells tore great holes in the walls. They also sawed out great jagged segments of the walls of both the convent and the church. The roof of the convent was knocked in, the greater part of it falling, as also did a considerable portion of the roof of the church. Nearly one-half of the walls of the convent were knocked off.

*Alamo Church Burned.*

Sometime after it had been repaired after the siege and capture of Santa Anna's army, the Alamo church was almost entirely destroyed by fire. This was along about the time of the Civil War. The convent portion escaped this visitation of conflagration, which did not therefore cause any change in the convent's appearance. The entire aspect of the church of the Alamo was changed when it was repaired after this fire. Originally towers surmounted the northwest and southwest corners of the church, these towers resembling those of the Concepción Mission. Its sweeping curved facade that now appears on the front was not there originally. Its roof was arched within, but flat on top.

There was no tower then on the convent building, but later the United States Quartermaster, while it was occupied as a warehouse, erected a room in the southwest corner of the convent and above the original walls which it surmounted. This room, which he used for his office, was reached by a stairway whose steps were placed on the southwest side of the convent building.

*Grenet Added the Second Story.*

When the convent property became the mercantile establishment of the late [Agustine] Honoré Grenet, he added the second story which is of lumber. He placed the present woodwork that forms it there. When he first built it, he put up a wooden turret above the second story's center. From this turret projected wooden cannon to give it a martial appearance that it never had possessed before. The room erected by the United States Quartermaster, whose name I believe was [James Harvey] Ralston, was made of stone. Its roof was shingled. Originally the large doors that occurred at frequent intervals along the west side of the convent building had carved arches above them. It was Grenet, I believe, who altered these to flat arches, as they now are. If the convent ever had towers, as the church had, they disappeared before I ever saw the structure.

Of course I do not mean to say what may have been the appearance of either the convent or the church before my memory and recollection of them commences. I do not question the statement of anyone regarding their appearance when first built. I have already appeared before a committee of the Texas Legislature and testified in regard to the appearance of both portions of the Alamo according to my first recollection of them. I do not now care to enter any controversy over the structure.

At the time the question of purchasing the church portion was pending I was living in Pleasanton. I was sent for to testify before a committee of the Legislature which was then investigating the matter and considering the purchase of the property. I do not know and never asked why the convent portion was not purchased when the purchase of the church portion was made, nor why the purchase of the convent was delayed until it was purchased by Miss [Clara] Driscoll, now Mrs. [Henry M.] Sevier, and when the shibboleth and slogan was: "Save the Alamo!"

Although I do not remember to have seen anyone killed in the convent because I was not in there when they were, I am told and believe that many of the defenders of the Alamo perished there.

*Taken Out of the Alamo.*

But to return to the story of the fall of the Alamo. After all of the men had been slain, the women and children were kept huddled up in the church's southwest corner in the small room to the right of the large double door of the church as one enters it. A guard was put over them. They were held there until after daylight when orders were given to remove them. We were all marched off to the house of Señor [Ramón] Músquiz. Here all of the women were again placed under guard. Músquiz owned a *suerte* [plot] on South Alamo Street not very far from where the Beethoven Hall now is. My mother and father were well acquainted with the Músquiz family. At about eight o'clock we became very hungry, up to then not having been given any food. My mother, being familiar with the premises, began to look about for food for herself and children as well as her other comrades. While she was doing so Músquiz told her that it was dangerous for her to be moving about and leaving the place and room in which she was under guard. She told him she did not care whether she was under guard or not, she was going to have something to eat for herself, her children and her companions whom she intended to feed if Santa Anna did not feed his prisoners. Músquiz admonished her to silence and told her to be patient and he would get them some food from his own store.

After urging my mother not to leave the room, Músquiz disappeared and went to his pantry, where he got quite a quantity of provisions and brought them to the room in which the prisoners, some ten or a dozen in number, were and distributed the food among them. There was some coffee as well as bread and meat. I recollect that I ate heartily, but my mother very sparingly.

We were kept at Músquiz's house until three o'clock in the afternoon when the prisoners were taken to Military Plaza.

*Esparza Before Santa Anna.*
We were halted on the plaza and in front of the place where Wolfson's store now is. Mrs. [Juana Navarro] Alsbury and her sister, Mrs. Gertrudes [Navarro] Cantú, were the first ones to be taken before Santa Anna. He questioned them and, after talking with them for a few minutes, discharged them from custody and they left. Mrs. Cantú afterwards removed to the Calaveras, where she married and resided up to the time of her death.

Mrs. [Susanna] Dickinson, the wife of Lieutenant [Almeron] Dickinson, the woman whom I told you, like my mother, had a babe at her breast, was the next to be summoned before Santa Anna. He spent some time in questioning her after which he dismissed her.

My mother was next called before the dictator. When she appeared before him my baby sister pressed closely to her bosom. I with my brother followed her into his presence. My brother was clinging to her skirt, but I stood to one side and behind her. I watched every move and listened to every word spoken. Santa Anna asked her name. She gave it. He then asked, "Where is your husband?"

She answered, sobbing: "He's dead at the Alamo."

Santa Anna next asked where the other members of the family were. She replied a brother of my father's, she was informed, was in his (Santa Anna's) army. This was true. My father had a brother whose name was Francisco Esparza, who joined the forces of Santa Anna. It was this brother who appeared before Santa Anna later and asked permission to search among the slain for my father's corpse. The permission was given. My uncle found my father's body and had it buried in the *campo santo* [cemetery] where Milam Square is now. I did not get a chance to see it before it was buried there as the burial, as all others incident to that battle, was a very hurried one. It is probable that my father was the only one who fought on the side of the Constitutionalists and against the forces of the dictator whose body was buried without having first been burned.

Santa Anna released my mother. He gave her a blanket and two silver dollars as he dismissed her. I was informed that he gave a blanket and the same sum of money to each of the other women who were brought from the Alamo before him.

I noticed him closely and saw he was the same officer I had seen dismount on the Main Plaza about sundown of the night when I went into the Alamo. After our release we went back to our home and my mother wept for many days and nights. I frequently went to the Main Plaza and watched the soldiers of Santa Anna and saw him quite a number of times before they marched away toward Houston where he was defeated. He had a very broad face and high cheek bones. He had a hard and cruel look and his countenance was a very sinister one. It has haunted me ever since I last saw it and I will never forget the face or the figure of Santa Anna.

*Charles Merritt Barnes*

*María de Jesús Delgado Buquor. San Antonio Express, 19 July 1907, 3, Library of University of Texas, San Antonio. Photograph taken by staff at Institute of Texan Cultures, San Antonio.*

- 27 -

María de Jesús Delgado Buquor
*San Antonio Express*
19 JULY 1907

*As a young girl, María de Jesús Delgado Buquor was in the town of San Antonio during the siege and fall of the Alamo. In this interview conducted after her eightieth birthday, she recalled details like the Mexican soldiers' harsh treatment of the townspeople and the rising smoke from the funeral pyre of the Alamo defenders.*

## WITNESSED LAST STRUGGLE
## OF THE ALAMO PATRIOTS
*Mrs. María de Jesús Buquor of Floresville Saw Fall of Cradle of Texas Liberty*
Warned Colonel Travis of Mexicans' Approach

To have witnessed the fall of the Alamo, that historic cradle of Texas liberty, and to have personally enjoyed the friendships of such men as Travis, Bowie and Crockett are honors such as few persons living today can boast and yet there is today down on the narrow little street of this city known as Arciniega a little, well-preserved Mexican woman who enjoyed the friendship of these men and who was in San Antonio when the death of Travis and his fellow heroes awakened Texas to a struggle that was to end only with the establishment of her freedom.

Mrs. M. J. Buquor, on the tenth of the past month, celebrated her 81st birthday and at the time of the fall of the Alamo was not quite ten years of age. Children in whose veins courses the warm blood of Castile, however, develop at an early age and Mrs. Buquor, in spite of her advanced age at present and her extreme youth at the time of the historic siege, is able to discourse in a very interesting manner concerning the incidents attendant upon the attack on the Texas stronghold by Santa Anna and the Mexican forces.

*Was Friend of Heroes.*

Sitting on the broad, old fashioned gallery of the house of her daughter, Mrs. Felicia Bledsoe of this city, whom she is here from Floresville to visit, and forming an interesting link between the present and the historic past, she yesterday related memories which rendered realistic the deeds which seem so unreal and far away when read in black and white. Her words transported one to the past and one seems to see Travis and Crockett at the home of her, who was then María de Jesús Delgado, on the day that Santa Anna marched to San Antonio. María de Jesús steps out into the yard and beholding many men approaching calls to her mother to question her concerning them. It is the Mexican army and Travis and Crockett hastily bid their friends farewell and hastened to the fortress and a glorious death.

Then Mrs. Buquor, for the little María de Jesús was she, gave Travis his first warning of the actual approach of the enemy although, of course, rumors of this enemy's coming had been heard for days. Mrs. Buquor says that this was not the last that she saw of the Texas patriots by any means as for days before the final onslaught by the Mexican troops Travis, Crockett and others of the garrison would wave greetings to their friends in this city and bid them good-by, knowing full well that their doom had been sealed and that death was very near.

During the siege Mrs. Buquor says she and her family as well as the other citizens suffered severe hardships and were harshly treated by the Mexican soldiers from whom they had no protection. The Delgado family, consisting of her mother, father, three sisters, four brothers and herself, she says was forced to give up their home, which is still standing on the river bank in the vicinity of the electric power house, to the Mexican soldiers. The members of the family sought refuge at the old Arciniega home which stood on the street which now bears his name. Here they were forced to dig and seek refuge in a cellar where they were safe from the bullets which swept the streets of the city at the moments of attack.

Childhood's idea of humor has not wholly departed from the now aged woman for she laughed slightly as she remembered the efforts of an aged, blind woman to get into the cellar and the woman's fall into the same just in time to avoid a bullet which whistled by.

*Santa Anna a Lothario.*
During the siege, Mrs. Buquor says she saw General Santa Anna many times and she bears testimony to his well known penchant for amours in that she related how he seized a young girl living near her home and held the maiden captive during his stay in the city.

She says that she did not see any of the Texas dead after the last final attack but she plainly remembers seeing the smoke arising from the burning bodies of the Texans when their remains were destroyed in this way, a sacrificial fire on the altar of Texas liberty. She, however, fails to remember much concerning the departure of the Mexican troops from the city.

Mrs. Buquor was born on June 10th, 1826, but it was not until 1830 that the family came to San Antonio. From 1830 until 1840 she remained in the city. In 1840 she married P[aschal] L[eo] Buquor . . . Twenty-two years ago he and his wife moved to Floresville at which place he died in 1900.

Mrs. Buquor has lived to see her family increased in size until, with the great-grandchildren, a small town would be filled by her descendants. With a laugh she said yesterday that she expected to live to see her great-great-grandchildren. She has two sons, John Buquor of El Paso and Adolph Buquor of this city, and two daughters, Mrs. Ophelia McLane of Calaveras and Mrs. Felicia Bledsoe of this city, alive, twenty grandchildren and did not know how many great-grandchildren. She is the only survivor of nine sisters and brothers who witnessed the fall of the Alamo.

She is well preserved, in spite of this numerous posterity, and her memory is wonderful considering her age. Save that she is a little confused as to dates, her memory is very clear. She related yesterday the death of seven Texans who tried to make their escape from the Alamo and were killed on the river bank near her house as vividly as if it were an event of the past few days.

*Juan Díaz. CN08091,*
San Antonio Light,
*1 September 1907, 13,*
*Texas Newspaper Collection,*
*Center for American History,*
*University of Texas, Austin.*

- 28 -
Juan Díaz
*San Antonio Light*
1 SEPTEMBER 1907

*Young Juan Díaz, whose father was the custodian of the local parish, San Fernando, watched from the church bell tower as Santa Anna's troops entered San Antonio. Later from the distant vantage point of the town he witnessed the Alamo battle and its aftermath. He also recollected the Mexican soldiers' treatment of the local populace. This newspaper interview occurred when Díaz was about eighty years old.*

## AS A BOY, JUAN DÍAZ, VENERABLE SAN ANTONIAN WITNESSED THE ATTACK ON THE ALAMO

When the sun rose Sunday morning, March 6, 1836, a little Mexican boy climbed the ladders that led to the tower of San Fernando Cathedral and watched the gorgeous forces of General Santa Anna as they marched into the city from the westward and halted on Main Plaza.

This mite of a boy who watched the invading forces come to San Antonio led by martial music and flying banners was Juan Díaz and he lives today at his home, 110 Speed Street, old and feeble, but still retaining vivid memories of that sabbath morning when the Mexican army came, the cannonading and subsequent capture of the Alamo, the slaughter of its defenders, and the final chapter, the burning of the dead on Alamo Plaza, out in front of where the Menger Hotel now stands.

Juan Díaz is the son of Antonio Díaz, who at the time of the fall of the Alamo was the trusted custodian of San Fernando Cathedral. The Díaz family lived near the church and young Juan played about the yard and the plaza. It was while he was playing with his sisters and some of the neighbor children that the sound of martial music broke on the air. Díaz says he was old enough to know something of what war meant and that the first thing he did was to send his sisters home. Then he scampered to the tower to watch the army, and later clambered down and stood in awe-struck wonder near the plaza as the big guns of the Mexicans began to roar and boom and send deadly cannon balls hurtling against the solid walls of the sacred Alamo.

"I will never forget how that army looked as it swept into town," said the old man as he told the story of what he knew and saw of the fall of the Alamo to a *Light* reporter yesterday. "At the head of the soldiers came the regimental band, playing the liveliest airs, and with the band came a squad of men bearing the flags and banners of Mexico and an immense image that looked like an alligator's head. The band stopped on Main Plaza and remained there until after the fall of the fort. The artillery was planted where the French Building now stands and the cannoneers had a clean sweep to the Alamo, for at that time there were no buildings between it and the San Fernando Cathedral."

Díaz tells how he watched the progress of the battle from a distant point of vantage, how, after the cannon had ceased to boom, he saw the six columns of Mexican soldiers form in line and go straight for the walls of the Alamo. He was not too far away to see the soldiers go scrambling up and up, only to be hurled back onto their comrades who, all undaunted, stepped into the breaches and fought their way to the top of the battle-scarred walls.

"I did not go to the plaza when the dead were burned," said Díaz. "I had no desire to see that great funeral pyre, but the odor of it permeated every part of the city. It was sickening and for weeks and months people shunned the Alamo. Some of the men who went there during the cremation told us that the Texas and Mexican soldiers were all piled in a heap and burned together."

Many of Santa Anna's staff officers had quarters at the San Fernando Cathedral and were fed by Díaz's mother. He says the general gave orders that their home was to be safe from the soldiers and that a guard was constantly on watch to see that no damage was done.

The aged Mexican says that for days after the battle there was the most intense excitement, but he asserts that Santa Anna kept his victorious soldiers well under control and that but few cases of damage resulted from their depredations.

Díaz was married at one time and was the father of several children. His wife died a number of years ago and now all the children have followed her to the grave. Díaz is a native of San Antonio and has lived here all his life. He is a charter member of the Mexican Society and is one of the very few original members of that association now alive. A large oil painting of the aged man hangs in Benevolencia Hall.

Díaz is still hale and hearty and says it is his desire to live to be more than one hundred years old.

*Juan Antonio Chávez.* CN08090,
*History of Southwest Texas, 1:452,*
*Center for American History,*
*University of Texas, Austin.*

- 29 -
Juan Antonio Chávez
*San Antonio Express*
15, 22 DECEMBER 1907

*Juan Antonio Chávez, who later held county and state elected offices, was a boy at the time of the Alamo battle. He abandoned San Antonio with his family before Mexican forces occupied the town. In this newspaper interview, Charles Merritt Barnes (see document 25) recorded a few details about the famous battle from the testimony of the eighty-year-old San Antonian.*

REMEMBERS EARLY DAYS
*Antonio Chávez Tells of the Old Military Plaza and the Many Things That Happened During and Following the Siege of the Alamo*

Among the very few who resided here when the tyrant, Santa Anna, made his incursions and created such havoc, is an old citizen whose home is at 229 Obrajo Street, within a very few yards of where he was born. This old resident is Don Juan Antonio Chávez, who was born in the year 1827. He was ten [nine] years old when the tyrant came and remembers it well. His parents were then living in the house where he was born. Speaking of the coming of Santa Anna, Don Antonio said:

When [Ben] Milam and his comrades came into San Antonio from the Molino Blanco, the December previous to the coming of Santa Anna, our home was right in the line of fire between Milam's men and the Mexican army under the command of General [Martín] Cos. On that occasion we were compelled to flee from home and seek refuge in the country. When we returned we found the house badly shattered with shot and shell. The doors were riddled with bullets and grape shot from the cannon and *escopetas* [muskets] and the rifle balls. Had our family remained some, if not all, would have been killed.

When Santa Anna was marching on San Antonio, a friend of my father's came and told us there was going to be another very wicked fight. He advised him to leave and go again into the country. The experience my father had during the previous fight between the forces of Milam and Cos induced him to heed the counsel of this friend. My father took the entire family with him to the country several miles away from the city. We remained there until the Alamo had fallen and all of its defenders slain. We did not return for quite a while afterward. This time our house was not in the line of fire, but we did not know this and it was much safer, anyway, for us in the country . . .

*Lived under Five Flags.*

I have lived in San Antonio under five different dominions and have seen as many flags float over her citadel and the Alamo since I have been living here. I was born under the Mexican dominion. Its constitutional flag of A.D. 1821, against which Santa Anna contended and prevailed, was floating over the Alamo when he came here in 1836. He captured it together with the Alamo and annihilated its brave defenders. On his arrival the flag he hoisted was the bloody red one. It was the flag of no country. He hoisted it to indicate his intention of giving no quarter.

*Charles Merritt Barnes*

- 30 -

Pablo Díaz
*San Antonio Light*
31 OCTOBER 1909

*This newspaper interview of the aging Pablo Díaz, conducted in English and Spanish, adds a few details to an earlier Díaz account (see document 25).*

## THIS MAN HEARD SHOTS FIRED AT BATTLE OF ALAMO
*Still Lives in San Antonio and Remembers Well Historic Fight—*
*Is 92 Years of Age*
Saw Bodies of Texas Heroes Burn

To have lived four score years and ten is the lot of few; to have been within earshot of the bombardment of the Alamo is given but to one man in San Antonio, Pablo Díaz, at 405 Tampico Street.

With rugged Aztec features, the bronzed face of the old man presents a picture which is indeed a character study. Alert and well preserved for a man thirty years his junior, at ninety-two years of age the old man still retains his faculties and walks with a step that is still firm beyond all belief, although his locks are silvered and his figure slightly stooping and bowed with age.

In a mixture of Spanish and English he tells the story of the bombardment and the fall of the Alamo. He tells of how he worked on the "Labor de Mission Concepción" for one Domingo Gusteos [Bustillos], he heard the terrible noise of "la guerra" (the war) as for eleven days the men of the Alamo defended their stronghold, the brave 176 Texans pitted against the four thousand Mexicans. A "hewer of wood and a drawer of water" was he, but Pablo Díaz was a witness to one of the greatest tragedies in the history of the world and lives to tell the tale of the great "guerra" to his children and his grandchildren.

When asked why he was not in San Antonio during the siege; why he continued to work in the "labor," he said, "No quiero la guerra" (I do not like war).

Going on with his story he tells how on the fateful morning of March 8 [March 6] at two o'clock began the last act in the terrible tragedy, when the Mexicans made a night attack upon the chapel and with crowbars and ladders scaled the walls and began the hand-to-hand encounter which ended in the massacre of all the brave little band who so desperately fought for their lives.

Then fell a great silence in the gray dawn, the fight was over and drawn by curiosity to learn what was the outcome of the "guerra," Pablo Díaz fared his way to San Antonio de Béxar and learned the details of the fall of the Alamo.

Forgetting then his English, he tells in Spanish, with words stumbling over each other in their liquid flow, how the Mexicans dragged branches of trees and limbs of trees through the streets and made a funeral pyre in the plaza off to the side of the Alamo. First a layer of wood and then a layer of corpses of the gallant Texans and then another layer of wood and then other corpses until the pyre was completed, Pablo Díaz declared was the work of Santa Anna, the Napoleon of the west.

When asked if he saw the flames which leaped to heaven consume their human sacrifice on the altar of liberty his voice trembled and tears gathered in his dim old eyes and he replied, "Sí, sí. No era bueno, no era bueno" (Yes, yes. It was not good; it was not good).

Pablo Díaz was born in Coahuila, Nuevo León, in 1817, and came to San Antonio when he was fourteen years old. He was nineteen years old when the fall of the Alamo took place and lived in a little house which stood where the French Building now is. After the battle of the Alamo he soon left working in the "labor" and he tells with pride how for forty-eight years he worked as a carpenter, working for many years for the elder Kampmann. As a humble workman he assisted in the building of many of the older buildings whose histories are woven into the warp and woof of old San Antonio.

For years he plied his vocation, sometimes going to Mexico, even as far as Coahuila, but returning always to his home in San Antonio. With pride he leads with tottering steps a short distance from his daughter's house and points to "mi propiedad" (my property), which consists of a large lot on which are built several small houses occupied by Mexican families. A land owner is he and a patriarch among his people, who listen with breathless interest to his tales of long ago and seek his advice with that reverence which Mexicans show to the aged.

- 31 -
Juan Vargas
*San Antonio Light*
3 APRIL 1910

*Mexican troops impressed Juan Vargas to serve in their camp, which was close enough to the Alamo for him to hear the sounds of the battle. Vargas was over a hundred years old when reporter Louis de Nette recorded his memories of the famous battle he witnessed from the distance.*

### THIS MAN WAS OLD WHEN SANTA ANNA SPILLED BLOOD IN ALAMO AND BUILT TEXANS' FUNERAL PYRE
*Juan Vargas of San Antonio Carries Weight of 114 Years*
Remembers Well Desperate Charge Against the Alamo

*Born January 1, 1796, twenty years after American Revolution, he has seen and participated in more historical events than any man alive—fought in 1810 for Mexican independence and in 1830 came to San Antonio to make his home. Five generations of the Vargas family are today alive, the youngest being Rosa, his three-year-old great-great-grandchild. His life and experiences related by himself.*

Juan Vargas, an Indian of the tribe from which Porfirio Díaz claims descent, a true descendant of the mighty Aztecs, is the man who has lived in three centuries and is now over 114 years old . . .

At the Alamo, that shrine, that altar bathed in heroes' blood and strewn with heroes' clay, Juan Vargas was not far distant. Impressed by Santa Anna, he was forced to menial tasks about camp and equipage. They did not force him to fight, for he refused to draw weapons against those with whom he had lived and his refusal almost cost him his life.

"Rivers of blood flowed," says the old man, now dim of mind in many things, but remembering the Alamo as though but yesterday. "Rivers of blood flowed and the earth ran red. Texans—Americans—gave their lives willingly to the holy cause. I—known as a Mexican and guarded by Santa Anna's men—bound up the wounds of the injured of his army and helped to bury the dead. My life is going. Little longer can I hope to keep this mold of clay animate; the grave, the crossing to the other side is before me, but over in eternity I shall carry with me the memory of that fight, of that struggle wherein the Alamo fell and Texan blood bedewed its floors." . . .

*Storming of the Alamo.*

Came rumors of war and then war Texans, chafing under the intolerable rule and despotism of Mexico, declared their independence. Santa Anna, conqueror and self-styled president of Mexico, sent his invincibles to down the spirit and slay the men who thus dared to affront him by seceding from the nominal state of the Republic of Mexico.

"I remember," says the aged man, "how the troops of Santa Anna marched into San Antonio de Béxar. I remember how they overawed all, taking what they wanted with no thought of pay. They had come to suppress a rebellion and one way to do it was to take the worldly goods of the rebels. They camped to uncounted numbers within the city, close to the Alamo and yet far enough away to escape the leaden hail which the Texans poured into them. As for me, I was with them. They had taken me in passing. I waited on them, performed kitchen and equipage tasks about camp. They said I did not know how to shoot and they would not trust me with a gun. Little did they know that I had fought with Padre [Miguel] Hidalgo and with [Agustín de] Iturbide.

"Things are dim to me now. As the light of day has gone from my eyes, so the light of memory has left my mind. But never can I forget the battle of the Alamo. I did not fire a shot, neither did I storm the old fort when the Mexicans rushed in to cut to pieces the last remnant of the gallant band. They did their own work, I refusing to go to the Alamo. For this they threatened execution when the day was won, but could not at that time waste a shell on me. One shell might mean victory or defeat. They used their shells on the Texans.

"Back in the camp I heard the roar of the artillery. Shriek of shell mingled with groan of dying; soldiers mutilated and torn stumbled into camp to be bound up; dozens and scores were dragged in with gaping wounds through which their lifeblood had trickled; ever and anon the cry of 'muerte a los Tejanos' [death to the Texans] echoed; carnage and a hell of battle reigned; Mexicans were mowed down as though a scythe passed; the uncounted dead were piled in camp, while [a] sort of service was rendered the living by doctors, aided by myself and others who, like me, had been impressed for this service.

"Oh, señor, that day is one to go down in history, for never did [a] patriot band go more willingly to death than did those handful of Texans imprisoned behind stone wall and fighting to the last. And never in history is there recorded a battle in which so few gave death to so many.

"The day after, the piling of those dead in trenches, the absence of humans from San Antonio—ah, but let us pass that, señor, let us pass that. I am old, close to the grave. Excitement is not good for me. I tremble and lose strength."

*Louis de Nette*

- 32 -

Enrique Esparza, Pablo Díaz, and Juan Antonio Chávez
*San Antonio Express*
26 MARCH 1911

*Charles Merritt Barnes interviewed Enrique Esparza, Pablo Díaz, and Juan Antonio Chávez (see also documents 25, 26, 29) and utilized their testimony for this newspaper account on the disposal of corpses after the Alamo battle.*

# BUILDERS' SPADES TURN UP SOIL BAKED BY ALAMO FUNERAL PYRES

*Site of Burial of Ashes of Travis and His Men Definitely Fixed*

Where workmen are excavating for the cellar of a new building that will stand on the spot of one of the two funeral pyres whereon the bodies of those slain in the Alamo's defense were consumed, is one of the memorable places of San Antonio, never marked and constantly passed unheeded. Few know that such a prominent event in history was there enacted. It will not be long before this spot and the one where the other funeral pyre was built will be the sites of buildings for commercial purposes and the populace, in all probability, will forget that either place was ever of such historical interest.

The spot where the cellar is being dug comprises one-half of the area on which the first pyre mentioned was located. It is on the north side of East Commerce Street, adjoining the Ludlow House. The building is being constructed by Dr. G[eorge] H[arrison] Moody. The pyre occupied a space about ten feet in width by sixty in length and extended from northwest to southeast from the property owned by Mrs. Ed Steves, on which the Ludlow House is built, to and through the property that the Moody structure is to occupy, and a short distance out into the street. The other pyre, which was of equal width, was about eighty feet long and was laid out in the same direction, but was on the opposite side and on property now owned by Dr. Ferdinand Herff, Sr., about 250 yards southeast of the first pyre, this property being known as the site of the old Post House or the Springfield House.

The sites of the two pyres have been pointed out to me by several persons, three of whom saw them when the bodies were being burned and before the ashes had been scattered and the fragments removed. These three persons are all living today. One of them is Enrique Esparza, who states he was a child eight years old when the siege and fall of the Alamo took place and that he was in the Alamo with his parents and one of his brothers. He said that his father and the brother mentioned were killed in the Alamo and his mother and he were taken before Santa Anna after it had fallen. Esparza says that Mrs. [Susanna] Dickinson, the wife of Lieutenant [Almeron] Dickinson, who became a mother during the siege and was taken with her infant to Santa Anna at the same time as also was Mrs. [Juana Navarro] Alsbury and several other women and children.

Santa Anna gave each of the women two silver pesos, or Mexican "dobe" dollars when he ordered their release. Esparza says:

After this we went to look for the body of my father and my brother, but when we got to the Alamo again all of the bodies had been removed and taken to the Alameda. They were put in two piles, one on each side of the Alameda, and burned. All of the dead killed in the siege who were defenders of the Alamo were burned, both Mexicans and Americans, and my father and brother were among them, but we could not find them in either pile, for the soldiers would not let us get close enough to examine or claim them.

They set fire to them and burned them. My mother placed her mantilla before her face and ran screaming from the scene, dragging me by the hand with her. After the bodies were burned we went back several times to the two places until all of the fragments had been removed and the ashes had been scattered in every direction.

### The Story of Don Pablo.

The next one to show me the two places was old Don Pablo Díaz, also still living, who said:

My parents fled with me. I was a child then. I had a brother older than I who espoused the cause of Santa Anna and fought in his army. After the Alamo had fallen we returned to town from the Calaveras, where we had gone. On our approach we saw a huge pillar of flames and smoke shooting up to a considerable height to the south and east of the Alamo. The dense smoke from this fire went up into the clouds and I watched it while the fire burned for two days and two nights. Then it subsided and smoldered. During this time we had been hiding in the southern part of the city and left our retreat, coming back to town by way of Garden Street.

I noticed that the air was tainted with a terrible odor from many corpses and that thousands of vultures were circling in the sky above us. They were hovering over the city and especially along and above the river's course. As I reached the ford of the San Antonio River at the old Lewis Mill site I encountered a terrible sight. The stream was congested with corpses that had been thrown into it.

[Francisco Antonio] Ruiz, the *alcalde* [mayor] at that time, had vainly striven to bury the dead soldiers of Santa Anna's command who had been slain in the struggle during the siege. After exhausting every effort and all of his resources, he was unable to give burial to but a very limited number, these principally being officers. Being unable to bury them in the earth he was compelled to dispose of them otherwise. He had them cast into the swiftly flowing stream. But they were so numerous that they choked up the stream, finding lodgement along the banks of the short curves and bends of that stream.

They obstructed the stream for some time until Ruiz was able to get a sufficient force to push the bodies away from the banks as they lodged against them and floated them down the stream for a considerable distance below, where they remained until devoured by the vultures and wolves.

I stopped and looked at the sickening sight, which made me shudder, and I became ill. I was told afterward that the sight and stench had even nauseated Santa Anna himself so that he had complained and reprimanded Ruiz for not getting rid of the dead. Involuntarily I put my hands before my eyes and turned away. But I could not, even then, help seeing the corpses. I turned away from the river which I hesitated to cross and went to the right along the settlement of La Villita, but even then could not help seeing the corpses, for they lined the river's course and banks all the way from Crockett Street to more than a mile below.

*Burning of the Bodies.*

But while the bodies of the Mexican soldiers in the river was a revolting spectacle the one that met my vision later was even more gruesome. It filled me with the greatest horror. I had passed along La Villita to South Alamo Street and thence north to the Alameda. This was a broad and spacious place used as a promenade and also as a highway of ingress to and egress from the city on the east side of the river. It has since become a part of East Commerce Street. On each side of the Alameda was a row of large cottonwood trees. From them the place took its name of Alameda. It commenced at about where St. Joseph's Church now stands, this having been the western extremity about half a block from South Alamo Street.

It was Santa Anna himself who had given orders to Ruiz to have the bodies of all who perished while defending the Alamo incinerated. By intuition I went straight to the place. I did not need a guide. The whole story was told by the spectacle I saw. The witnesses were silent but eloquent ones. They were the charred skulls, fragments of arms, hands, feet and other members of the bodies of the dead defenders. In carts the slain, among whom were Travis, Crockett, Bowie, [James Butler] Bonham and [Green B.] Jameson, as well as all of the others, had been removed from the Alamo mission, where they fell, to the Alameda, where they were burned on two different pyres. These were about 250 yards apart and one was on each side of the Alameda. The one on the north side was the smallest, while that on the south side was the largest. The latter was probably about twenty feet longer than the former. Both were about the same width—about eight or ten feet. Both pyres were about ten feet high when the flames were first kindled and the consuming of the corpses commenced.

In alternate layers the corpses and wood were placed. Grease of different kinds, principally tallow, was melted and poured over the two pyres. They were then ignited and burned until they burned out, leaving but a few fragments of different members. Most of the corpses were entirely consumed.

When I reached the spot I saw ashes, as well as the blackened chars of the different anatomical fragments. They emitted an odor even more sickening than did the corpses of those who had been thrown into the river and to me were much more nauseating.

*Third Eyewitness.*
Don Juan Antonio Chávez, also living here now, who saw the remnants of the pyres and the fragments of the bodies, was the third eyewitness who showed me the same spots that the other two did and confirmed their stories, all three coinciding.

Antonio Pérez and August Biesenbach also showed me the same places and stated they had been the ones whereon the bodies had been burned . . .

There was an orchard very near the place where the bodies were burned on the south side of the Alameda and it is stated that flames and sparks blowing in the fierce March wind that prevailed a part of the time during the incineration blew the flames into the orchard, injuring many and destroying some of the fruit trees, most of which died soon after.

This fact probably gave rise to the prevalent belief that obtained for many years, that after the bodies were burned none of the fruit trees in the neighborhood would bear and that they as well as the cottonwood trees all died soon after.

It is a fact that there are now no bearing fruit trees within a block of where either of the two pyres were and there are but two of the fifty or more cottonwood trees left that grew originally on the Alameda. Neither of them is within a block of either of the pyres.

*Charles Merritt Barnes*


- 33 -

Juan Díaz, Enrique Esparza, and Juan Antonio Chávez
*San Antonio Express*
27 AUGUST 1911

*Charles Merritt Barnes interviewed Juan Díaz, Enrique Esparza, and Juan Antonio Chávez for a newspaper account on local history which included brief recollections of the Alamo battle. Barnes recorded the testimony of Esparza and Chávez in previous articles (see documents 26, 29, and 32), but a San Antonio Light reporter wrote the only earlier published account based on the recollections of Díaz (see document 28).*

## MEN STILL LIVING WHO SAW THE FALL OF THE ALAMO

Juan Díaz, who states he is 105 years old and was born in old Mexico, but came to San Antonio before the siege of the Alamo, saw the memorable combat there between the heroes who defended the historic pile and the troops under Santa Anna. Díaz says he watched the burning of the bodies of those slain in the Alamo. He saw them placed on two pyres on the old Alameda, which is now East Commerce Street . . . Not long ago he sat for the *Express* staff artist, who took the picture of him that appears on this page. While quite decrepit, he still gets around and is frequently found on the streets, talking in Spanish about old times . . .

### Is an Interesting Citizen.

Enrique Esparza, not quite a nonagenarian, but nearing the ninety-year mark, is perhaps the most interesting of all of the Mexican aged citizens. He makes claim to having been in the Alamo during the siege of that celebrated group. There is no doubt that his father and one of his brothers perished there, as their names appear on the roll of the slain. He states that he and his mother, who were in there during the combat, escaped slaughter, she on account of her sex and he on account of his tender youth, he being at that time under ten years of age. He details the episodes incident to the memorable combat and those that transpired subsequent to it. He vividly describes the circumstance of his mother and himself being taken before Santa Anna, together with several other women and children, among the former being Mrs. [Susanna] Dickinson, wife of Lieutenant [Almeron] Dickinson, and Mrs. [Juana Navarro] Alsbury. He also saw the incineration of the bodies of those slain during the defense of the Alamo and says they were burned on the Alameda. Old as he is, Esparza cultivates a small tract of land. He has a son and several daughters, as well as numerous grandchildren and great-grandchildren.

Don Juan Antonio Chávez is another aged San Antonian, nearly ninety years old, who has spent the greater part of his life either in San Antonio or on the Calaveras Creek, in which locality he has a fine ranch. He was in San Antonio when Santa Anna and his soldiers entered and left the city with his parents when the siege commenced, going to the ranch. He returned during the time the bodies were being burned and saw the ashes and remnants of the pyres as well as some skulls, arms and other fragments of humanity that had not been entirely consumed.

*Charles Merritt Barnes*

- 34 -
Trinidad Coy
As Recalled by His Son Andrés Coy
*San Antonio Light*
26 NOVEMBER 1911

*Trinidad Coy's amazing story was reported in a newspaper interview of his son Andrés, a local policeman. The younger Coy recollected that his father was one of several scouts sent from the Alamo to ascertain Santa Anna's position and intentions. He was a prisoner in the Mexican camp as the battle raged in the distance.*

## NEW LIGHT ON ALAMO MASSACRE

*Trinidad Coy Sent Out on Reconnaissance, Might Have Been Able to Avert Disaster Had His Horse Been Less Partial to Loco Weed— Information Which Colonel Travis Needed to Formulate Better Plan Never Came.*

But for the unguarded action of a farmer's boy, the history of Texas and the map of the United States might today be different.

When Travis, Bowie and Crockett and their band of immortal heroes lay intrenched in the Alamo in April [February] 1836, rumors flew about that Santa Anna and his Mexican troops were on the way to San Antonio. There was no way to trace these reports to any authentic source. But their very persistency gave rise to suspicion and credence in the minds of the brave Texans.

As a consequence, Travis, who was at that time in command of the troops at the Alamo, sent out scouts who were to locate the Mexicans under Santa Anna, if possible, and to bring in accurate information as to their whereabouts, and their probable destination. If it were possible, the scouts were to bring in an estimate of the probable force of the Mexican troops, so that action might be taken in accordance with the information so secured.

There is living today a descendant of one of the scouts, from whom this information has been secured. Some of it sheds a new light on the situation that finally culminated in the massacre in the historic little mission on the plaza in San Antonio.

Police Captain Andrés Coy is the son of one of the messengers sent out by Colonel Travis.

### Intelligence Needed.

According to the story told to Captain Coy by his father, the command under Colonel Travis believed that they were unable to withstand a concerted attack by the Mexican army, if it were true that Santa Anna really was headed towards San Antonio.

Plans were being discussed as to the advisability of resisting the attack or of moving out of San Antonio for the purpose of augmenting the forces available for actual fighting. There was considerable discussion, until finally Davy Crockett, who wanted to be right before he went ahead, proposed a plan.

"If it is true that Santa Anna is coming to San Antonio," he said, "then our plans must be made one way. If he is not coming to San Antonio, they must be made another way. The proper thing to do is to find out whether he is coming to San Antonio. Isn't that so? Well, let's send out men to find out where he is and what he intends to do."

The suggestion met with instant approval from Travis and from Bowie, who was listening to the conversation from his cot in the next room, where he lay ill. So it was decided to send out a reconnaissance party to locate the army of Mexicans under Santa Anna and to discover their probable destination.

### Goes on Reconnaissance.

Among the men sent on this errand was Trinidad Coy, father of the present police captain. He mounted his horse and faced to the south, in an attempt to follow the trail of rumor that led from San Antonio back to the Mexican forces.

As he proceeded on his way the scent grew warmer. Day by day he became convinced that there was truth in the rumor, that Santa Anna was on his way to the city of San Antonio. Several times he was sent off on a cold trail—he traveled roads that led him farther and farther from his quest. Then he would retrace his way and pick up the trail where he had left it.

He was without news from home. Days had passed now and he was without the least intimation that would lead him to believe that he should continue his quest. By day he would ride and ride, stopping now and then to inquire the latest news of a farmer, or to verify a report that had come to him further up the road. Sometimes he passed hours without seeing a human being.

Then, when he had stopped for the night and was rolling a cigarette at the home of some lone farmer, or when the coals of his campfire glowed brightly in the clear nights, he would begin to wonder whether, after all, he had better not give up the search and return to San Antonio.

### In a Quandary.

Coy was a brave man. He knew that Travis' forces were inadequate to withstand any attack from a great force. He knew the tremendous importance of the coming battles and realized the need Travis had of every possible rifleman.

The thought distressed him. He was not of the calibre that prefers to be a spectator of events. His was the tribe that chose rather to do, when there was need of men of action. The problem was a hard one.

If Travis had need of him in San Antonio, if one of the other men had arrived with news of the actual approach of the Mexican troops, then his place was in San Antonio. And without loss of time he would present himself before his commander, prepared to take whatever orders the commander might choose to give.

If, though, none of the other men had been able to obtain news of the invaders, and if Coy was on the track of real news of such importance, it was his plain duty to work out his string to the end and to come back with the news that these men so anxiously awaited.

There were no telegraphs in those days in Texas. News could reach him from Colonel Travis only by means of another messenger. If there was no danger of an attack by Santa Anna's army, there would be no need to send word to Coy. If there were danger of such an attack the garrison could not afford to send a messenger. For one able to deliver such a message was able to bear a gun in the fight for independence.

So Coy knew he would not hear from Travis. He knew his orders and they were plain and distinct. He was to find the Mexican army and report its strength, its whereabouts and its probable destination to Travis. That was all. If he performed this task and ill came of it, the fault was surely not his.

### Great News Comes.

But this staunch old fighter did not view the matter in this light. If there was going to be fighting and he was needed, he was going to be present. He determined to spend three more days in the search and then retrace his steps, unless he had some urgent reason to continue on his way.

For two days there was the same story of conflicting information. Farmers along the road had heard that the Mexicans were approaching. They had been hearing this for some weeks. They had no authentic information. They had merely heard the rumor when they met other men on the road at the little market towns. No one positively knew anything. Coy became disheartened. He decided to return. He made plans to go to San Antonio the next day.

Then, while the men were smoking silently after supper, a neighbor came in with great news. The Mexicans were close by. They had made camp for the night only a few miles down the road.

They were on their way to San Antonio. At last the fact was assured.

Coy called the farmer's son to him and ordered that his horse be saddled at once. Cautioning his friends not to disclose the fact of his presence or his mission he mounted and started to ride away. His horse was unwilling. Here was a new and astonishing difficulty. The sturdy cow pony that had never failed him in any emergency now refused to move. While Coy was pondering the situation the horse sank to his knees and lay down.

*Loco Weed.*
"He has been eating something," said Coy. Turning to the farmer's boy, he inquired, "What have you given my horse?"

"Nothing," answered the boy.

"But you did," insisted Coy. "What was it?"

"Nothing," repeated the boy. "I just turned him into the corral to graze and threw him some hay."

The farmer spoke up. "Into which corral did you turn him? The big one?"

"Yes, sir."

"Fool! Did you not know that you had thrown there all the loco weed that came in from the wagons today?"

The boy hung his head. "I forgot," he said.

While the boy went for one of the farmer's horses to take the place of the sick animal, the father explained that he had sent wagons out into the fields that day to gather grasses and hay for fodder and that much of the dreaded loco weed had been found among it. The dangerous weed had been separated and thrown into the big corral, where the animals could not get to it. While he was apologizing for the boy's carelessness, the youngster came back leading a wiry little pony. Coy appraised the animal's strength and stamina. Then, apparently satisfied, he mounted and sped on his way to give the warning.

Now, if ever, he must be sure. Now, if ever, must his speed be great, his caution true, his judgment certain. The fate of Texas hung on his hands. Could he reach the mission in San Antonio in time? He whipped up his horse to a swifter gallop.

*Discovered.*

"Halt!"

The word rang out in the night like a pistol shot. Voices followed it and Coy recognized the Mexican accent. These must be scouts or outposts of Santa Anna's army. He dug the spurs into his horse and flew down the road.

"Halt!"

Again the command stung the ears of the flying Texan. He only pressed forward the harder. Behind him on the road he heard the patter of many hoofs in hard pursuit.

Oh, for the little trusty pony now, whose feet were so true, whose chest so deep, whose endurance untiring. Hard, indeed, the fate that caused him to become poisoned on such a night! Then, with horror, Coy noticed that his horse was failing him. Its head sagged, its steps were staggering and blind. He whipped it up, he drove the cruel spurs deep into the quivering side. The horse threw up its head and with a last gasp of speed, jumped forward a pace or two and fell forward—dead.

The pursuers were hard behind him. Coy dodged into the brush. He heard the soldiers stop in the road where had fallen his horse, heard the quick command to scatter and find him in the brush. He crawled on hands and knees away from his pursuers. Then, from nowhere, a Mexican soldier jumped upon his back and called for help. In another moment he was a prisoner.

Called before the commander of the little troop, he explained that he was on his way to a neighboring little town to see a sick sister, that he was in no way connected with the Texas army, that all he desired was permission to depart unmolested.

The Mexican commandant pondered awhile. "Well," he decided, "you may be telling the truth. But I believe that you ate some of the loco weed that you fed to your horse there in the road. You come with us."

*Too Late.*

They carried him back to the main army. With them, as a prisoner, he was taken to San Antonio. One day they appeared before the city. Coy afterwards learned that their appearance was entirely unexpected. The defenders were taken by surprise.

He was kept in the Mexican camp while preparations were made to attack the band of faithful heroes in the little church. With great avidity he saw the work go forward that was to destroy his comrades, to whom he should have brought word. He cursed the luck that had tied his hands in this important of all important hours.

The preparations of warfare went on. The attack commenced. With unholy joy, he saw the Mexican troops beaten back, only to surge forward again, overpowering the brave defenders by sheer weight of numbers. He longed to join his friends.

Looking hastily about him he saw that the camp was deserted. All the hangers-on had followed the line of soldiery. He worked his bonds against a stone until they parted. He made his way out of the camp, followed a well-known path that led around the city, and in another hour he had arrived at a point in back of the chapel of the Alamo, from where he could join his comrades.

Only a bank of cottonwood trees hid them from his view. He forced his way through the underbrush. The Alamo lay before him. There were no signs of fighting. All was quiet. Only, before his eyes, there rose the heavy black cloud from a smoking pile.

It was the funeral pyre of his friends.

*José María Rodríguez.* CN08093, Rodríguez Memoirs of Early Texas *(San Antonio: Passing Show Printing, 1913; reprint, San Antonio: Standard, 1961), frontispiece. Courtesy Center for American History, University of Texas, Austin.*

- 35 -

José María Rodríguez
*Rodríguez Memoirs of Early Texas*
1913

*José María Rodríguez was a boy during the Alamo battle and abandoned San Antonio during the siege and final assault. Rodríguez was from a prominent San Antonio family and later was active in local politics. His* Memoirs, *written and published at the end of his distinguished career, recounts events in San Antonio before and after the battle, as well as the young Rodríguez's observations from the distant rooftop of a house during the battle itself.*

Shortly after that [the Texan capture of San Antonio in December 1835], Colonel Travis was put in command with a small garrison and he stayed at the Alamo. Colonel Travis was a fine looking man of more than ordinary height. I recollect him distinctly from the very fact that he used to come up to our house from the Alamo and talk to my father and mother a great deal. Our house was the first one after you crossed the river coming from the Alamo and Colonel Travis generally stopped at our home going and coming. He was a very popular man and was well liked by everyone. My father was always in sympathy with the Texas cause, but had so far not taken up arms on either side.

Soon after this, a report came to my father from a reliable source that Santa Anna was starting for San Antonio with seven thousand men composed of cavalry, infantry and artillery, in fact a well organized army. My father sent for Colonel Travis and he came to our house and my father told him about this coming of Santa Anna and advised him to retire into the interior of Texas and abandon the Alamo. He told him he could not resist Santa Anna's army with such a small force. Colonel Travis told my father that he could not believe it, because General [Martín] Cos had only been defeated less than three months and it did not seem possible to him that General Santa Anna could organize in so short a time as large an army as that. Colonel Travis, therefore, remained at the Alamo and at the last Travis told my father, "Well we have made up our minds to die at the Alamo fighting for Texas." My father asked him again to retire as General Sam Houston was then in the interior of Texas organizing an army.

The Mexicans in San Antonio who were in sympathy with the war of independence organized a company under Colonel Juan Seguín. There were twenty-four in the company including my father and they joined the command of General Sam Houston. My mother and all of us remained in the city.

One morning early a man named [Cayetano?] Rivas called at our house and told us that he had seen Santa Anna in disguise the night before looking in on a *fandango* [dance] on Soledad Street. My father being away with

General Houston's army, my mother undertook to act for us and decided it was best for us to go into the country to avoid being here when General Santa Anna's army should come in. We went to the ranch of Doña Santos Ximenes. We left in ox carts, the wheels of which were made of solid wood. We buried our money in the house, about eight hundred dollars; it took us nearly two days to get to the ranch.

A few days after that, one morning about daybreak, I heard some firing and Pablo Olivarri, who was with us, woke me up. He said, "You had better get up on the house; they are fighting at the Alamo." We got up on the house and could see the flash of the guns and hear the booming of the cannon. The firing lasted about two hours. The next day we heard that all the Texans had been killed and the Alamo taken. A few days after that an army consisting of about twelve hundred men under General [José] Urrea came by from San Antonio on their way to Goliad to attack [James Walker] Fannin. I saw these troops as they passed the ranch.

There has been a great deal of discussion with reference to what had been done with the bodies of the Texans who were slain in the Alamo. It is claimed that Colonel Seguín wrote a letter in which he stated that he got together the ashes in the following February and put them in an iron urn and buried them in San Fernando Cathedral. This does not seem possible to me because nothing of that kind could have happened without us knowing that and we never heard of any occurrence of that kind. Seguín did not return from Houston's army until my father did, both of them being in the same command, my father a first lieutenant and he a colonel. It is true that the bones were brought together somewhere in the neighborhood or a little east of where the Menger Hotel is now and were buried by Colonel Seguín, but that any of them were ever buried in the cathedral, I have never heard nor do I believe that to be true . . .

About eight months after the battle of San Jacinto, the company in which my father served was mustered out and he was honorably discharged. While he was still in the army, a brother of my mother's came to Washington [-on-the-Brazos] and brought us back to San Antonio and my father after leaving the army returned to San Antonio and went to merchandising.

Two or three days after we got to San Antonio, I went to the Alamo and saw the blood on the walls.

Juan Antonio Chávez
*San Antonio Express*
19 APRIL 1914

*This interview of Juan Antonio Chávez adds to earlier Chávez accounts (see documents 29, 32, and 33) by describing in greater detail the disposal of corpses after the Alamo battle.*

## BULLET-RIDDEN AND TOMAHAWK-SCARRED
## SAN ANTONIO HOME IS BEING DEMOLISHED

Speaking of the old Chávez home, the first house in San Antonio captured by [Ben] Milam and his men, the late Don [Juan] Antonio Chávez once said:

When that battle occurred [the December 1835 Texan siege of San Antonio] I was a small boy, but I remember the circumstances well. As soon as it began my father left with all our family and went to our ranch on Calaveras Creek, about fifteen miles from this city, and we remained there in safety until the fighting was over. When we returned home the house was almost a ruin. The walls had wide rents in them made by the cannon shot. In them were many bullet holes and marks and the doors and windows had been pierced and riddled.

We did not remain tranquilly at home very long. Profiting by our former experience and as advised by numerous friends, my father on the approach of Santa Anna's forces again left the house two and a half months later and went back to the ranch, where we remained until the siege of the Alamo was over. When we returned the bodies of those that had perished in the Alamo were still burning on two immense pyres on the old Alameda. I went to look at them and the sight indelibly impressed itself upon my memory. One pyre occupied a position on the site of where the new Halff building is. The other was diagonally across the street on what is now known as the lawn of the Ludlow House and the recently built house adjoining it on the east. The bodies burned for several days and the wood and tallow fuel used for consuming them was frequently replenished. I made several trips to the scene, which so fascinated me I could not stay away until all of the bodies had been consumed. They were all reduced to ashes except a few charred heads, arms, and legs that were scattered about. These were gathered up and placed in a shallow grave where the Ludlow House lawn now is.

All of the officers and some of the privates of Santa Anna's army, according to Don [Juan] Antonio Chávez, were buried in the cemetery where Milam Park now is, but the slain Mexicans were so numerous it was thought the quickest and best way of getting rid of the bodies was by throwing them in the San Antonio River, then a swift and deep stream. There were so many bodies they choked its flow. Many of them lodged in the curves of the river.

*Antonio Menchaca. CN07387, Antonio Menchaca file, Prints and Photographs Collection, Center for American History, University of Texas, Austin.*

- 37 -

Antonio Menchaca
*Memoirs*
1937

*Antonio Menchaca, a Texas veteran of the San Jacinto battle, left San Antonio with his family before the Mexican army occupied the town. Local journalist James P. Newcomb recorded some reminiscences of the elderly Menchaca during the 1870s, providing the text for a later published version, Menchaca's Memoirs. Memoirs includes narration of some events in San Antonio before the arrival of Santa Anna's advancing army.*

On the 26th December 1835, Don Diego [James] Grant left San Antonio towards Matamoros with about five hundred men, Americans and Mexicans of those who had assisted in the siege [of San Antonio]. They here kept up guards and patrols of night. Two hundred fifty men went from here to keep a lookout on [Mexican general Martín] Cos, who had gone to Mexico, and returning here on the 5th January 1836.

On the 13th January 1836, David Crockett presented himself at the old Mexican graveyard on the west side of the San Pedro Creek, had in company with him fourteen young men who had accompanied him from Tennessee here. As soon as he got there he sent word to Bowie to go and receive him and conduct him into the city. Bowie and Menchaca went and he was brought and lodged at Erasmo Seguín's house. Crockett, Bowie, Travis, [James Clinton] Neill and all the officers joined together to establish guards for the safety of the city, they fearing that the Mexicans would return.

On the 10th February 1836, Menchaca was invited by officers to a ball given in honor of Crockett and was asked to invite all the principal ladies in the city to it. On the same day invitations were extended and the ball given that night. While at the ball, at about one o'clock A.M. of the 11th, a courier sent by Placido Benavides arrived from Camargo with the intelligence that Santa Anna was starting from the Presidio [de] Rio Grande with thirteen thousand troops, ten thousand infantry and three thousand cavalry, with the view of taking San Antonio. The courier arrived at the ball room door, inquired for Colonel Seguín, and was told that Colonel Seguín was not there. Asked if Menchaca was there and was told that he was. He spoke to him and told him that he had a letter of great importance which he had brought from Benavides from Camargo, asked partner and came to see letter. Opened letter and read the following: "At this moment I have received a very certain notice that the commander in chief, Antonio López de Santa Anna, marches for the city of San Antonio to take possession thereof, with thirteen thousand men." As he was reading letter, Bowie came opposite him, came to see it, and while reading it, Travis came up and Bowie called him to read that letter; but Travis said that at that moment he could not stay to read letters, for he was dancing with the most beautiful lady in San Antonio. Bowie told him that the letter was one of grave importance and for him to leave his partner. Travis came and brought Crockett with him. Travis and Bowie understood Spanish, Crockett did not. Travis then said it will take thirteen thousand men from the Presidio de Rio Grande to this place thirteen or fourteen days to get here; this is the fourth day. Let us dance tonight and tomorrow we will make provisions for our defense. The ball continued until seven o'clock A.M.

There Travis invited officers to hold a meeting with a view of consulting as to the best means they should adopt for the security of the place. The council gathered. Many resolutions were offered and adopted, after which Bowie and Seguín made a motion to have Antonio Menchaca and his family sent away from here, knowing that should Santa Anna come, Menchaca and his family would receive no good at his hands. Menchaca left here and went to Seguín's ranch, where he stayed six days, preparing for a trip . . . Menchaca continued his journey, got to Gonzales, at the house of G[reen] DeWitt and there met up with General Edward Burleson, with seventy-three men, who had just got there, then slept. And on the following day, attempted to pass to the other side with families, but was prevented by Burleson, who told him that the families might cross, but not him; that the men were needed in the army. There met up with fourteen Mexicans of San Antonio and they united and remained there until a company could be formed. The Americans were gradually being strengthened by the addition of from three to fifteen daily. Six days after being there Colonel Seguín, who was sent as courier by Travis, arrived there and presented himself to General Burleson who, upon receipt of the message, forwarded it to the Convention [for Texas Independence] assembled at Washington [-on-the-Brazos], Texas.

In a recent essay, anthropologist Richard Flores recounted his first visit to the Alamo. Accompanied by his third grade classmates, Flores was filled with awe as he imagined the heroic deeds of Texas legends like Bowie, Travis, and Crockett, whom he had learned were martyrs for freedom. These musings were abruptly interrupted after leaving the mission church, however, when Flores' best friend Robert nudged him and whispered, "You killed them! You and the other 'mes'kins'!" Flustered, the young Flores retorted that he had never killed anyone, nor had his grandfather, whom he perceived as the most likely contemporary of the Alamo battle among his relatives. But this defense did not shield him from the enduring influence of his friend's accusation. Flores concluded: "I don't know what I lost that day, if it was innocence, certitude, identity, or some other existentially derived nine-year old sense-of-self. Whatever it was, it was gone."[1]

Flores' experience during his first visit to the Alamo reflects that of other Mexican Americans. The popular perception of the Alamo battle as a conflict between barbaric Mexican savages and heroic Anglo-American martyrs is amazingly persistent. Fortunately, this perception is fading in light of the historical fact that women and men of Mexican heritage served within the Alamo during the siege and final assault. Yet, even for Mexican Americans who are enlightened about Tejano defenders of the Alamo, the famous battle can remain an ambiguous historical event. Historian Rodolfo Acuña, for example, stated upon resigning from the advisory board of a 1982 Public Broadcasting Service program on Texas Revolutionary hero Juan Nepomuceno Seguín: "To make heroes of the Mexican people defending the Alamo is like making heroes of the Vichy government . . . *Seguín* represents an accommodationist point of view that promotes the wrong kind of assimilation."[2]

The statements of Flores and Acuña reveal the dilemma which many Mexican Americans face with regard to the Alamo. To identify with the victorious Mexican army leaves Mexican Americans open to the false accusation Flores' friend Robert leveled at him: that they descend from a race of murderous butchers who are the enemies of liberty. But to identify with Tejano Alamo defenders implies that their ancestors rejected their own people and heritage to ally themselves with Anglo-American aspirations and ideals.

Tejano accounts of the Alamo are important records for Mexican Americans who face this dilemma. While various historical works examine the Mexican and Texan viewpoints on the famous battle, extant Tejano accounts suggest a third perspective. Unlike African Americans, Anglo Americans, European immigrants, and Mexican soldiers who fought at the Alamo, San Antonians of Mexican heritage were hometown residents caught between two opposing armies. Like many of today's Mexican Americans, nineteenth-century Tejanos felt pressured to choose between their Texas homeland and their Mexican cultural motherland. Collectively, their accounts are a legacy of the hometown Tejano perspective often forgotten in our remembrance of the Alamo.

The diverse vantage points from which San Antonio Tejanos observed the Alamo battle reflect their response to the dilemma of choosing sides in the conflict between Mexico and Texas. Tejanos who witnessed the battle from within the Alamo cast their lot with the Texan troops. Juan Seguín and Trinidad Coy espoused the Texan cause by serving as courier and scout, respectively. Whether willingly or forcedly, most Tejanos who stayed in the town assisted General Antonio López de Santa Anna and the Mexican army. Their counterparts who fled the town until the end of the hostilities remained neutral or at least delayed the decision about which side they would support.

Some San Antonio families were split in the difficult choice between opposing armies. Gregorio Esparza fought for Texas in the 1835 siege of San Antonio and in the Alamo, while his brother Francisco was in the Mexican army. The Rodríguez and Navarro families were also divided in their loyalties.[3]

Although friends, neighbors, and even families were divided among the forces of Mexico, the forces of Texas, and the stance of neutrality, all three groups continued to form an amazingly cohesive community at San Antonio. At times this bond among hometown residents even transcended social class divisions within the local populace. According to Enrique Esparza, after the battle his mother agreed not to tell Santa Anna that Juana Melton was married to an Anglo American, even though Mrs. Melton "was considered an aristocrat" and "had never recognized my mother as an acquaintance." Tejano Alamo reminiscences also indicate that residents who fled the town during the hostilities returned without recrimination and that families with conflicting allegiances during the war were quickly reunited. For example, although Francisco Esparza enlisted in the Mexican army which his brother Gregorio opposed to the death, he arranged for Gregorio's burial immediately after the battle. Later he testified on behalf of Gregorio's family in their petition for a land claim as heirs of an Alamo defender. This is one of at least five land claim files in which Tejanos who assisted the Mexican army provided sworn depositions for the families of Tejano Alamo defenders. Francisco Esparza's own petition for a land claim included a deposition from Antonio Menchaca, even though they fought in opposing armies during the war.[4]

The harmony among San Antonio Tejanos was further illustrated in the first municipal elections under the Republic of Texas, when an overwhelmingly Tejano electorate chose candidates who had assisted the Mexican forces during the war, along with others who had supported the Texan cause. Despite their previous conflicting loyalties, local leaders and that same Tejano populace also participated harmoniously in the interment ceremony for the Alamo defenders.[5] Significantly, while some Tejano Alamo accounts condemn the brutality of Santa Anna and the Mexican army and a few criticize the deeds of Anglo-American officers and soldiers, in none of these accounts do San Antonio Tejanos deride one another for their actions and divergent allegiances during the conflict.

These signs of unity among San Antonio Tejanos reflect their history as a relatively homogeneous group of settlers on the northern frontier of New Spain (and later Mexico). They also reflect Tejano response to the dilemma of choosing sides during the Texas Revolution. Although some local Tejanos supported the Mexican or Texan sides, apparently their strongest allegiance was to their fellow San Antonians with whom they shared a common history and a common plight as war was waged in their hometown. Consciously or not, this group allegiance of San Antonio Tejanos shaped their identity as a people distinct from their Mexican counterparts south of the Rio Grande and from their Anglo-American neighbors in Texas. As theologian Virgilio Elizondo has stated, for Tejanos and their descendants, "The Alamo was not a defeat and it was not a victory[,] but it was a painful birth of a new people."[6]

Tejano Alamo accounts are significant for Mexican Americans who face an ongoing dilemma with regard to the Alamo. As it did their nineteenth-century ancestors, the Alamo has presented contemporary Mexican Americans the difficult choice of identifying with their cultural roots or with the land of their birth. As was previously mentioned, Richard Flores refused to accept the stereotypical view that the Alamo illustrates the inherent savagery of the Mexican people, while Rodolfo Acuña rejected as accommodationist the more recent exaltation of Tejano Alamo defenders. Their reluctance to identify completely with either the Alamo's attackers or its defenders mirrors the earlier collective response of San Antonio Tejanos. Tejano Alamo accounts record this collective response, a response which illuminates the Alamo's importance for Mexican-American consciousness and ethnic identity.

NOTES

1. Richard R. Flores, "Memory-Place, the Alamo, and the Construction of Meaning," *American Journal of Semiotics*, forthcoming.

2. As cited in Susan Prendergast Schoelwer with Tom W. Gläser, *Alamo Images: Changing Perceptions of a Texas Experience*, with a foreword by Clifton H. Jones and an introduction by Paul Andrew Hutton (Dallas: DeGolyer Library and Southern Methodist University Press, 1985), 7. For a further treatment of contemporary Tejano response to the Alamo, see Holly Beachley Brear, *Inherit the Alamo: Myth and Ritual at an American Shrine* (Austin: University of Texas Press, 1995); Edward Tabor Linenthal, *Sacred Ground: Americans and Their Battlefields* (Urbana: University of Illinois Press, 1991), 70–78; Arnoldo de León, "Tejanos and the Texas War for Independence: Historiography's Judgment," *New Mexico Historical Review* 61 (April 1986): 137–146.

3. Francisco Esparza, Deposition, 26 August 1859, Court of Claims Voucher File #2558, General Land Office, Austin (GLO), [document 11]; Enrique Esparza, interviewed in "Another Child of the Alamo," Adina De Zavala, *San Antonio Light*, 10 November 1901 [23]; Enrique Esparza, interviewed in "The Story of Enrique Esparza," *San Antonio Express*, 22 November 1902 [24]; Enrique Esparza, interviewed in "Alamo's Only Survivor," Charles Merritt Barnes, *San Antonio Express*, 19 May 1907, 47 [26]; Enrique Esparza, interviewed in "Alamo's Fall Is Told by Witness in a Land Suit," *San Antonio Express*, 9 December 1908, 20; J[osé] M[aría] Rodríguez, *Rodríguez Memoirs of Early Texas* (San Antonio: Passing Show Printing, 1913; reprint, San Antonio: Standard, 1961), 15–16; "Señor Navarro Tells the Story of His Grandfather," in *Rise of the Lone Star: A Story of Texas Told by Its Pioneers*, ed. Howard R. Driggs and Sarah S. King (New York: Frederick A. Stokes, 1936), 268–269, 272–273; R[euben] M. Potter, *The Texas Revolution: Distinguished Mexicans Who Took Part in the Revolution of Texas, with Glances at Its Early Events*, 18 (reprinted from the *Magazine of American History*, October 1878); Paul D. Lack, *The Texas Revolutionary Experience: A Political and Social History, 1835–1836* (College Station: Texas A&M University Press, 1992), 165.

4. Esparza, interviewed in "The Story of Enrique Esparza" (quotations); Francisco Esparza, Deposition; Enrique Esparza, interviewed in "Another Child of the Alamo," De Zavala; Esparza, "Alamo's Only Survivor," Barnes, 19 May 1907, 47; Esparza, interviewed in "Esparza, the Boy of the Alamo, Remembers," in *Rise of the Lone Star*, ed. Driggs and King, 229; Court of Claims Voucher File #2558, 1858, 1859 (heirs of Gregorio Esparza), GLO; Court of Claims Voucher File #5026, 1861 (heirs of Toribio Losoya), GLO; Court of Claims Voucher File #6073, 1856, 1860 (heirs of Andrés Nava), GLO; Carlos Espalier File, 1855, 1856, Memorials and Petitions, TSA; Damacio Jiménez File, 1861, Headright Book 2, 370–373, ABCC; Court of Claims Voucher File #2557, 1860, GLO. Citing Enrique Esparza, a 1911 account claims that Gregorio Esparza's body was never found and consequently was burned with other fallen Alamo defenders. This claim contradicts earlier testimony by several witnesses, including Enrique Esparza himself. Barnes, "Builders' Spades Turn Up Soil Baked by Alamo Funeral Pyres," *San Antonio Express*, 26 March 1911.

5. The 1837 electees to San Antonio municipal offices included city treasurer Eugenio Navarro, who remained loyal to Mexico during the war,

for example, and councilman Francisco Antonio Ruiz, the former mayor, who assisted Santa Anna with the disposal of bodies after the battle. On the other hand, John William Smith, an Alamo defender who escaped death because he left the fortress as a courier, was elected mayor. Smith was the only Anglo American in a field of forty-one candidates. "Minutes of the City Council of the City of San Antonio from 1837 to 1849, Journal A" (typescript), 3–5, Center for American History, University of Texas, Austin. These election results are also summarized in Fane Downs, "The History of Mexicans in Texas, 1820–1845" (Ph.D. diss., Texas Tech University, Lubbock, 1970), 255–256. At the interment ceremony for the Alamo defenders, Texas veteran Colonel Juan Seguín led the proceedings and gave a patriotic speech. Seguín's official report of this ceremony indicates that local clergy also participated. At the time, Father Refugio de la Garza was San Antonio's pastor. Unlike Seguín, De la Garza was loyal to the Mexican cause. Juan Seguín to General Albert Sidney Johnston, 13 March 1837, Johnston Papers, Howard Tilton Memorial Library, Tulane University, New Orleans, [3]; *Columbia* (later *Houston*) *Telegraph and Texas Register*, 28 March, 4 April 1837, [4]; Timothy M. Matovina, *Tejano Religion and Ethnicity: San Antonio, 1821–1860* (Austin: University of Texas Press, 1995), 42. Seguín's speech and letter are also in *A Revolution Remembered: The Memoirs and Selected Correspondence of Juan N. Seguín*, ed. Jesús F. de la Teja (Austin: State House Press, 1991), 156, 161–162.

6. Virgilio P. Elizondo, *Colección Mestiza Americana* (San Antonio: Mexican American Cultural Center Press, 1975), 108–109. Elizondo's statement echoes the inscription on the Plaza de las Tres Culturas in Mexico City. For the development of San Antonio Tejano identity, see Gerald E. Poyo and Gilberto M. Hinojosa, eds., *Tejano Origins in Eighteenth-Century San Antonio* (Austin: University of Texas Press, 1991); Matovina, *Tejano Religion and Ethnicity*.

# BIBLIOGRAPHY

Abbreviations Used

ABCC   Archives, Béxar County Courthouse, San Antonio
CAH    Center for American History, University of Texas, Austin
DRT    Daughters of the Republic of Texas Library, San Antonio
GLO    General Land Office, Austin
TSA    Texas State Archives, Austin


Unpublished Sources

Barrera, Agustín. Deposition, 26 July 1856. Carlos Espalier File, Memorials and
      Petitions. TSA.
————. Deposition, 16 April 1861. Court of Claims Voucher File #5026 (heirs of
      Toribio Losoya). GLO.
Barrera, Agustín, and Manuel López. Deposition, 1 January 1856. Antonio Fuentes
      File, Memorials and Petitions. TSA.
Casanova, Remigio. Deposition, 29 October 1874. Pension File of Brigidio
      Guerrero, Republic Pension Applications. TSA. Brigidio Guerrero's affidavit
      and other documents in this file recount Guerrero's services to Texas but do
      not mention his participation in the Alamo battle.
Cormona, Cesario. Deposition, 22 November 1860. Court of Claims Voucher
      File #6073 (heirs of Andrés Nava). GLO.
Cruz Arocha, Antonio. Statement, no date. Gentilz Papers. DRT.
Curvier y Losoya, María Francisca. Petition, 16 April 1861. Court of Claims Voucher
      File #5026 (heirs of Toribio Losoya). GLO.
De los Reyes, Damasio. Deposition, 4 September 1856. Court of Claims Voucher
      File #6073 (heirs of Andrés Nava). GLO.
Delgado, Cornelio. Deposition, 22 November 1860. Court of Claims Voucher
      File #6073 (heirs of Andrés Nava). GLO.

———. Deposition, 30 March 1861. Headright Book 2, 371–372, Damacio Jiménez File. ABCC.

Esparza, Francisco. Deposition, 26 August 1859. Court of Claims Voucher File #2558 (heirs of Gregorio Esparza). GLO.

———. Petition, 24 August 1860. Court of Claims Voucher File #2557 (Francisco Esparza). GLO.

Flores, Manuel. Deposition, 13 December 1858. Court of Claims Voucher File #2558 (heirs of Gregorio Esparza). GLO.

García, Juan. Deposition, 4 January 1861. Court of Claims Voucher File #3416 (Brigidio Guerrero). GLO.

Gómez, Francisco. Deposition, 24 August 1860. Court of Claims Voucher File #2557 (Francisco Esparza). GLO.

Gongora, Carmel. See Muñoz, Doroteo, and Carmel Gongora.

Granada, Francisco, and Juan A. Urutia. Deposition, 26 July 1856. Carlos Espalier File, Memorials and Petitions. TSA.

Guarde Grande, Luz. Petition, 5 October 1855. Carlos Espalier File, Memorials and Petitions. TSA.

Guerrero, Brigidio. Petition, 4 January 1861. Court of Claims Voucher File #3416 (Brigidio Guerrero). GLO.

Hernández, Gregorio. Deposition, 27 December 1858. Court of Claims Voucher File #2558 (heirs of Gregorio Esparza). GLO.

Jiménez, Gertrudes. See Jiménez, Juan, and Gertrudes Jiménez.

Jiménez, Juan, and Gertrudes Jiménez. Petition, 2 February 1861. Headright Book 2, 370, Damacio Jiménez File. ABCC.

López, Manuel. See Barrera, Agustín, and Manuel López.

Martínez, Gabriel. Petition, 1 January 1850. Memorials and Petitions. TSA.

Menchaca, Antonio. Deposition, 1 January 1856. Antonio Fuentes File, Memorials and Petitions. TSA.

———. Deposition, 28 July 1856. Carlos Espalier File, Memorials and Petitions. TSA.

———. Deposition, 24 August 1860. Court of Claims Voucher File #2557 (Francisco Esparza). GLO.

Muñoz, Doroteo, and Carmel Gongora. Petition, 21 November 1860. Court of Claims Voucher File #6073 (heirs of Andrés Nava). GLO.

Muñoz, Eugenio. Deposition, 5 January 1861. Court of Claims Voucher File #3416 (Brigidio Guerrero). GLO.

Navarro [Alsbury], Juana. Deposition, 23 October 1855. Carlos Espalier File, Memorials and Petitions. TSA.

———. Petition, 1 November 1857. Memorials and Petitions. TSA.

Rivas, Cayetano. Deposition, 26 July 1856. Carlos Espalier File, Memorials and Petitions. TSA.

Ruiz, Francisco [Antonio]. Deposition, 22 October 1855. Carlos Espalier File, Memorials and Petitions. TSA.

———. Deposition, 16 April 1861. Court of Claims Voucher File #5026 (heirs of Toribio Losoya). GLO.

Seguín, Juan N. Deposition, 22 November 1860. Court of Claims Voucher File #6073 (heirs of Andrés Nava). GLO.

———. Deposition, 2 February 1861. Headright Book 2, 371, Damacio Jiménez File. ABCC.

Urutia, Juan A. See Granada, Francisco, and Juan A. Urutia.

Villanueva, Candelario. Deposition, 26 August 1859. Court of Claims Voucher File #2558 (heirs of Gregorio Esparza). GLO.


Published Sources


Barcena, Andrés. See "Examination of Andrés Barcena and Anselmo Bergara"; Gray, E. N.; Houston, Sam.

Barnes, Charles Merritt. "Builders' Spades Turn Up Soil Baked by Alamo Funeral Pyres." *San Antonio Express*, 26 March 1911, 26. Reprinted in Donald E. Everett, *San Antonio Legacy*. San Antonio: Trinity University Press, 1979, 98–100.
Enrique Esparza, Pablo Díaz, and Juan Antonio Chávez recollect the disposal of corpses after the Alamo battle.

———. *Combats and Conquests of Immortal Heroes: Sung in Song and Told in Story*. San Antonio: Guessaz & Ferlet, 1910, 218, 227, 231.
Recollections of Juan Antonio Chávez, Enrique Esparza, and Juan E. Barrera.

———. "Men Still Living Who Saw the Fall of the Alamo." *San Antonio Express*, 27 August 1911, 9.
Recollections of Juan Díaz, Enrique Esparza, and Juan Antonio Chávez.

Barrera, Agustín. "Mexicans Who Fell in the Alamo," 184–?. In *The Papers of Mirabeau Buonaparte Lamar*, ed. Charles Adams Gulick, Jr., and Katherine Elliott, 6:297. Austin: Von Boeckmann-Jones, 1973.
Historical note that lists five Tejano Alamo defenders.

Barrera, Juan E. See Barnes, Charles Merritt, *Combats and Conquests of Immortal Heroes*.

Bergara, Anselmo. See "Examination of Andrés Barcena and Anselmo Bergara"; Gray, E. N.; Houston, Sam.

Bollaert, William. *William Bollaert's Texas*, ed. W. Eugene Hollon and Ruth Lapham Butler, 222–224. Norman: University of Oklahoma Press, 1956.
Conversations with two local Tejanos about the Alamo.

Castañón Villanueva, Andrea (Madam Candelaria). "Alamo Massacre." Interview in *San Antonio Light*, 19 February 1899, 6. Reprinted in Maurice Elfer, *Madam Candelaria: Unsung Heroine of the Alamo*. Houston: Rein, 1933.

———. "Fall of the Alamo." Interview in *San Antonio Express*, 6 March 1892, 6.

———. "The Last Survivor of the Alamo, Señora Candelaria." Interview by Lee C. Harby, *Times-Democrat* (New Orleans), 22 April 1894, 28.

———. "The Last Voice Hushed." Interview in *San Antonio Express*, 11 February 1899, 5.

———. "Señora Candelaria." Interview in *San Antonio de Béxar: A Guide and History*, ed. and comp. William Corner. San Antonio: Bainbridge & Corner, 1890; reprint, San Antonio: Graphic Arts, 1977, 117–119.

———. See also Ford, John S., "The Alamo's Fall: A Synopsis of the Display of Heroism"; "The Fall of the Alamo"; *Origin and Fall of the Alamo March 6, 1836*.

Chávez, Juan Antonio. "Bullet-Ridden and Tomahawk-Scarred San Antonio Home Is Being Demolished." Interview in *San Antonio Express*, 19 April 1914, B45.

———. "Remembers Early Days." Interview by Charles Merritt Barnes, *San Antonio Express*, 15 December 1907, 54; 22 December 1907, 11.

———. See also Barnes, Charles Merritt, "Builders' Spades Turn Up Soil Baked by Alamo Funeral Pyres"; *Combats and Conquests of Immortal Heroes*; "Men Still Living Who Saw the Fall of the Alamo."

Coy, Trinidad. "New Light on Alamo Massacre." Interview of his son Andrés Coy in *San Antonio Light*, 26 November 1911, 41.

De la Teja, Jesús F., ed. *A Revolution Remembered: The Memoirs and Selected Correspondence of Juan N. Seguín*. Austin: State House Press, 1991, 79–81, 107–108, 156, 161–162, 191–195.

Statements regarding the Alamo by Juan N. Seguín from his memoirs, correspondence, and a newspaper article.

Delgado Buquor, Maríde [María de] Jesús. "Witnessed Last Struggle of the Alamo Patriots." Interview in *San Antonio Express*, 19 July 1907, 3.

Díaz, Juan. "As a Boy, Juan Díaz, Venerable San Antonian Witnessed the Attack on the Alamo." Interview in *San Antonio Light*, 1 September 1907, 13.

———. See also Barnes, Charles Merritt, "Men Still Living Who Saw the Fall of the Alamo."

Díaz, Pablo. "Aged Citizen Describes Alamo Fight and Fire." Interview by Charles Merritt Barnes, *San Antonio Express*, 1 July 1906, 11.

———. "This Man Heard Shots Fired at Battle of Alamo." Interview in *San Antonio Light*, 31 October 1909, 10.

———. See also Barnes, Charles Merritt, "Builders' Spades Turn Up Soil Baked by Alamo Funeral Pyres."

Esparza, Enrique. "Alamo's Fall Is Told by Witness in a Land Suit." Interview in *San Antonio Express*, 9 December 1908, 20.

———. "Alamo's Only Survivor." Interview by Charles Merritt Barnes, *San Antonio Express*, 12 May 1907, 14; 19 May 1907, 47.

———. "Another Child of the Alamo." Interview by Adina de Zavala, *San Antonio Light*, 10 November 1901, 9. Also appeared as "Children of the Alamo." *Houston Chronicle*, 9 November 1901, 4.

———. "Esparza, the Boy of the Alamo, Remembers." In *Rise of the Lone Star: A Story of Texas Told by Its Pioneers*, ed. Howard R. Driggs and Sarah S. King, 215, 220–230. New York: Frederick A. Stokes, 1936.

———. "The Story of Enrique Esparza." Interview in *San Antonio Express*, 22 November 1902, 8. Reprinted as "Story of the Massacre of Heroes of the Alamo." *San Antonio Express*, 7 March 1904, 5.

———. See also Barnes, Charles Merritt, "Builders' Spades Turn Up Soil Baked by Alamo Funeral Pyres"; *Combats and Conquests of Immortal Heroes*; "Men Still Living Who Saw the Fall of the Alamo."

"Examination of Andrés Bárcena and Anselmo Bergara," Gonzales, 11 March 1836. In *The Papers of the Texas Revolution, 1835–1836*, ed. John H. Jenkins, 5:45–46. Austin: Presidial, 1973. Also in *Texas Letters*, ed. Frederick C. Chabot, 146–147. San Antonio: Yanaguana Society, 1940.

Ford, John S. "The Alamo's Fall: A Synopsis of the Display of Heroism." *San Antonio Express*, 6 March 1889, 2.
Brief summary of statements about the Alamo battle by Andrea Castañón Villanueva, Juana Navarro Alsbury, and Francisco Antonio Ruiz.

———. "The Fall of the Alamo." *Dallas Morning News*, 12 November 1892, 6.
Brief summary of statements about the Alamo battle by Andrea Castañón Villanueva and Juana Navarro Alsbury.

———. *Origin and Fall of the Alamo March 6, 1836*. San Antonio: Johnson Brothers, 1895, 22.
Brief summary of statements about the Alamo battle by Andrea Castañón Villanueva, Juana Navarro Alsbury, and Francisco Antonio Ruiz.

Gray, E. N., to [?], 11 March 1836 (typescript), Republic of Texas General File. CAH. Published in *The Papers of the Texas Revolution, 1835–1836*, ed. John H. Jenkins, 5:48–49. Austin: Presidial, 1973.
Statements of Andrés Barcena and Anselmo Bergara.

Houston, Sam, to James W. Fannin, 11 March 1836. In *The Papers of the Texas Revolution, 1835–1836*, ed. John H. Jenkins, 5:52–54. Austin: Presidial, 1973. Also in *The Writings of Sam Houston, 1813–1863*, ed. Amelia W. Williams and Eugene C. Barker, 1:362–365. Austin: University of Texas Press, 1938; reprint,

Austin: Pemberton, 1970.

Statements of [Andrés Barcena] and Anselmo Bergara.

Maverick, Mary A. "Fall of the Alamo." In *Samuel Maverick, Texan: 1803–1870. A Collection of Letters, Journals, and Memoirs*, ed. Rena Maverick Green, 55–56. San Antonio: Privately printed, 1952.

Synopsis of a conversation with Juana Navarro Alsbury regarding her experience during the Alamo battle.

Menchaca, Antonio. *Memoirs*. With a foreword by Frederick C. Chabot and an introduction by James P. Newcomb. San Antonio: Yanaguana Society, 1937, 22–23.

A slightly different rendering of this text is in "The Memoirs of Captain Menchaca, 1807–1836" (typescript), ed. and annot. James P. Newcomb, 3–7. CAH. The original of Menchaca's memoirs is also at CAH, although it lacks the pages cited here. This original document is not dated, but precedes Menchaca's death in 1879.

Navarro Alsbury, Juana. "Mrs. Alsbury's Recollections of the Alamo," c. 1880s. In "John S. Ford Memoirs" (unpublished manuscript), 102–104. CAH.

Included among published accounts in this collection because, like many published Alamo accounts, it is a relatively extensive narrative obtained by an interviewer.

———. See also Ford, John S., "The Alamo's Fall: A Synopsis of the Display of Heroism"; "The Fall of the Alamo"; and *Origin and Fall of the Alamo March 6, 1836*; Maverick, Mary A., "Fall of the Alamo."

Navarro, José Antonio. In Josiah Gregg, *Diary and Letters of Josiah Gregg*, ed. Maurice Garland Fulton, with an introduction by Paul Horgan, 1:232. Norman: University of Oklahoma Press, 1941.

Rodríguez, J[osé] M[aría]. *Rodríguez Memoirs of Early Texas*. San Antonio: Passing Show Printing, 1913; reprint, San Antonio: Standard, 1961, 7–9, 16, 71. Also in "Six Year Old Boy Saw Alamo Fall." Interview in *San Antonio Express*, 21 June 1927, A10.

———. "Stirring Events Are Remembered by Texas Jurist." Interview in *San Antonio Express*, 8 September 1912, 35.

Ruiz, Francisco Antonio. "Fall of the Alamo, and Massacre of Travis and His Brave Associates." In *The Texas Almanac for 1860*, trans. J[osé] A[gustín] Quintero, 80–81. Houston: James Burke, 1859. Also in *The Texas Almanac, 1857–1873: A Compendium of Texas History*, comp. James M. Day, with an introduction by Walter Moore, 356–358. Waco: Texian Press, 1967. See also *Alamo Express* (San Antonio), 25 August 1860, 1.

———. See also Ford, John S., "The Alamo's Fall: A Synopsis of the Display of Heroism"; *Origin and Fall of the Alamo March 6, 1836*.

Seguín, Juan Nepomuceno. Address at the interment ceremony for the Alamo defenders. *Columbia* (later *Houston*) *Telegraph and Texas Register*, 4 April 1837. Also in *A Revolution Remembered*, ed. De la Teja, 156.

———. "Colonel Juan N. Seguín." Interview in *Clarksville Standard*, 4 March 1887. Also in *A Revolution Remembered*, ed. De la Teja, 191–193.

———. Letter to General Albert Sidney Johnston, 13 March 1837. Johnston Papers, Howard Tilton Memorial Library, Tulane University, New Orleans. Published in *A Revolution Remembered*, ed. De la Teja, 161–162.

———. Letter to Hamilton P. Bee, 28 March 1889. TSA. Published in *A Revolution Remembered*, ed. De la Teja, 193; *San Antonio Express*, 21 April 1889, 3.

———. Letter to William Winston Fontaine, 7 June 1890. W. W. Fontaine Collection. CAH. Published in *A Revolution Remembered*, ed. De la Teja, 194–195.

———. *Personal Memoirs of John N. Seguín, from the Year 1834 to the Retreat of General Woll from the City of San Antonio in 1842.* San Antonio: Ledger Book and Job Office, 1858, 8–10. Also in *A Revolution Remembered*, ed. De la Teja, 79–81, 107–108.

Vargas, Juan. "This Man Was Old When Santa Anna Spilled Blood in Alamo and Built Texans' Funeral Pyre." Interview by Louis de Nette, *San Antonio Light*, 3 April 1910, 34.

Yorba, Eulalia. "Another Story of the Alamo." Interview in *San Antonio Express*, 12 April 1896, 13.

no buildings between it and the
    Alamo, 94
red flag hoisted over, 74
Santa Anna dismounts in front
    of, 79
watch kept on tower of, 50
*San Francisco Examiner*, 54
San Jacinto, battle of, 19, 36, 48–49,
    115, 117
San Pedro Creek, 34, 67, 118
San Sabá, 25
Santa Anna, Antonio Lopez de
    Alamo survivors sent before, 6,
        46, 66, 71–72, 87–89, 102–103,
        107, 123
    allows Francisco Esparza to bury
        his brother, 71, 88
    allows Gonzales reinforcements
        to enter Alamo, 51
    armistice and conferences with
        Crockett, 70, 81
    army of encircles Alamo, 49, 51,
        54–55, 59
    army of goes to interior of Texas,
        34, 89
    arrival at San Antonio, 12n.13,
        34–35, 41, 43, 50, 54, 59, 65, 68,
        74, 79–80, 90, 92–93, 95, 100,
        107
    assumes dictatorship of Mexico,
        74
    attempt to let Alamo defenders
        depart in peace, 3, 27, 70, 81
    Barcena and Bergara accused of
        being spies of, 18
    Bergara remains in San Antonio
        thirteen days after arrival of, 18
    Bowie and Seguín recommend
        Menchaca family depart before
        arrival of, 119
    claims he kept his soldiers under
        control at San Antonio, 7, 94
    commences bombardment of
        Alamo, 50
    comments on brutality of, 25, 64,
        75, 82, 123
    conquest of Alamo mentioned, 32,
        37, 86, 90, 96
    cuts off water in Alamo ditch, 69,
        84
    demands surrender of Alamo
        garrison, 80
    deriding jeers from troops of, 80
    and disposal of Mexican corpses
        after battle, 4, 42–44, 75, 103–
        104, 117, 126n.5
    Enrique Esparza observes soldiers
        of, 89
    enters Alamo after battle, 27
    exploits young woman at San
        Antonio, 7, 48, 91
    first reports that he took the
        Alamo, 1, 17–18
    fortifications made in preparation
        for arrival of, 7, 74
    Guerrero claims he tried to join
        forces of, 83
    hoists red flag from San Fernando
        Church, 74
    mentioned, 31, 99, 106, 117
    observation that he had more
        troops than he could use, 71
    officers of quartered at San
        Fernando Church, 94

mentioned, 4, 32, 34, 70, 90

Navarro Alsbury left in care of,
45

opposes Seguín's appointment as
courier, 51

orders burning of Martínez
house, 31

personal observations on, 77, 114

physical appearance of, 114

place where he died pointed out,
2–3, 25

posts guard for safety of San
Antonio, 118

Rodríguez advises to retreat, 7,
114

sends couriers for reinforcements, 41, 49–51, 81, 119

sends scouts to locate Mexican
army, 108

site where body burned, 76, 102,
105

warned of Mexican army's
approach, 90–91, 114, 118

watch of confiscated, 46

within the walls of the Alamo,
54, 81, 85, 91, 108–110, 114

witnesses identify corpse of, 35,
37, 43–44